A

PRACTICAL TREATISE ON THE CULTURE

OF THE

CARNATION,

PINK, AURICULA, POLYANTHUS, RANUNCULUS,
TULIP, HYACINTH, ROSE, AND
OTHER FLOWERS:

WITH A

DISSERTATION ON SOILS AND MANURES, AND CATALOGUES
OF THE MOST ESTEEMED VARIETIES OF EACH FLOWER.

By THOMAS HOGG, Florist,

PADDINGTON GREEN, MIDDLESEX.

‘ The Flower Garden is an endless Source of Pleasure.’
‘ Si quid novisti rectius istis,
Candidus imperti, si non, his utere mecum.’

Sixth Edition.
WITH COLOURED ILLUSTRATIONS.

LONDON:
WHITTAKER & CO., AVE-MARIA-LANE.
1839.

Printing Statement:

Due to the very old age and scarcity of this book,
many of the pages may be hard to read due to the
blurring of the original text, possible missing pages,
missing text, dark backgrounds and other issues
beyond our control.

Because this is such an important and rare work, we
believe it is best to reproduce this book regardless of
its original condition.

Thank you for your understanding.

———

TO THE

RIGHT HONOURABLE

DOWAGER LADY DE CLIFFORD.

———

MAY IT PLEASE YOUR LADYSHIP,

It is with no small degree of satisfaction that I here record your Ladyship's permission to introduce this small and humble work to public notice, under the sanction of your Ladyship's distinguished name; believe me, I am duly sensible of the honour conferred, as well as of the powerful recommendation which it thereby receives.

Your Ladyship's name, I may fairly say, is in a manner identified with the science of botany itself; for you have been its liberal and munificent patroness for years, and have long pursued it, as a study at once innocent,

rational, and amusing, with unwearied ardour and success.

The various productions of Nature which you have
collected from all parts and all climates of the world,
some requiring the fostering warmth of the stove, others
the more temperate atmosphere of the green-house,—to
say nothing of those that adorn the open garden,—each
distinguished for some striking and peculiar property,
either of elegant and stately growth, curious and remarkable foliage, or beautiful and odoriferous blossom,
whether tree, shrub, or herb, bespeak alike your Ladyship's refined taste and judicious selection.

I am,

With sentiments of profound respect,

Your Ladyship's most obliged,

And most grateful servant,

THOMAS HOGG.

Paddington Green.

PREFACE

TO THE SECOND EDITION.

———

THE liberal encouragement which the former Edition of this little Work has met with from the admirers of the Flower-garden in general, as well as from the skilful and experienced Florist, has enabled the Author to put forth a Second Edition, in which he has made very considerable additions, and introduced a variety of new matter connected with the subject, being the result of two years' additional experience and information. He has added, under their respective heads, full, yet concise and amended, catalogues of each Flower treated of. Those of the Rose, of the Hyacinth, of Geraniums, of Herbaceous Plants, of annual Flowers, are new, and he hopes will prove acceptable; all which he has endeavoured to compress into as small a compass as possible, having inserted only what appeared both essential and needful. Five new Plates have been added, to illustrate the properties of a good flower;

the expense of which, and the superior manner in which this Edition has been got up, will, he hopes, justify the additional charge put upon the book.

He cannot let pass this opportunity of returning his most grateful thanks to those Ladies and Gentlemen, who have not only recommended and patronized his small Treatise, but who have still more essentially served him by the purchase of his flowers; his Collection of which, he begs to assure them, as long as his health or circumstances will admit, will always be found to be choice, curious, and extensive, and the charge also will be as moderate as that of any other Florist.

Paddington.

NOTE BY THE PUBLISHERS.

———

THE Publishers of this Edition of Hogg's Treatise on Flowers, which has so closely followed the preceding, beg leave to state that all the additions, corrections, and improvements made by the Author himself in the last, are carefully retained in this; so that they now present it to the Public as complete in every respect, and worthy of the very liberal patronage it has already received.

Ave-Maria Lane,
Aug. 1832.

INTRODUCTION.

As the hand of an all-beneficent Creator
has been graciously pleased to strew and decorate the earth with flowers, to gratify the
sight by their beauty, and to refresh the sense
of smelling by their fragrance, as we proceed
from stage to stage along the rugged road of
life; and as nothing which he has formed for
the benefit of man was ever designed by him
to perish or exist in vain, it is our duty to
receive these pleasing productions of his,
among others, with all thankfulness, and to
render them subservient to the purposes of
health, pleasure, and amusement; for such
no doubt he first bestowed them. In fact, the
cultivation of flowers has in all parts, as well

as in all ages of the world, engaged more or less the care and attention of a great part of mankind; for the same Being that created them, created in man also a wish and an inclination to cultivate and take charge of them. To spend too much of our time upon them may be justly deemed folly; yet not to notice them at all shows a corrupted taste, and a total want of grateful sensibility.

While they contribute to charm the eye by their gay external appearance, they furnish at the same time, to the intelligent mind of man, matter for study and reflection. The operations of nature in the vegetable world are most wonderful, both in the production and preservation of her numerous progeny, whether we contemplate their endless diversity, their curious construction, their varied foliage, their beautiful blossoms, their fragrance, their different stages of existence, and terms of duration, perennial, biennial, annual. These, and a hundred other remarkable pro- perties, cannot fail to engage our study and excite our curiosity: whether we direct our attention to the humble Lily of the Valley, or to the more magnificent blossom of the Magnolia, still we find something to admire, something to astonish and delight us.

> ' Go mark the workings of the power
> That shuts within the seed the future Flower;
> Bids these in elegance of form excel,
> In colour these, and those delight the smell;
> Sends Nature forth, the daughter of the skies,
> To dwell on earth, and charm all human eyes.'
>
> COWPER.

To take a view for a moment of the larger productions of nature—and though the fre- quency of beholding those objects, however wonderful, never fails to lessen the interest which we should otherwise feel, if the sight of them were not so familiar—yet who can

pass by the stately Elm, the towering Beech,
the lofty Fir, or the sturdy outstretched
branches of the majestic Oak, without having
his astonishment and admiration excited?
But how would that wonder and astonishment increase, if he had an opportunity of
beholding the immense Cedars growing on
their native mountains of Libanus, the stu-
pendous Icaria on the sides and summits of
the Andes, and the stately Palms of India, to
say nothing of the Norwegian Pines, or the
lofty Poplars that grow along the banks of
the Po in Lombardy!

To enter upon the description here, or to
enumerate the various uses and properties of
those gigantic productions of Nature, those
prodigies of vegetable life, which constitute
the pride and ornament of the forest, would
carry me too far from my subject; I will
therefore proceed to take a cursory view of

the less noble and majestic, but more beautiful and attractive inhabitants of the Flower Garden—enter but which, the restless and turbulent passions which disturb and agitate the breasts of men, amidst the busy and active pursuits of life, subside into a calm, and give place to the milder and softer emotions of the soul: everything here is calculated to inspire serenity and delight; Nature here offers an inexhaustible fund of amusement, not confining it to one single day, or week, or month, but to almost every day, week, and month in the year,—still increasing, varying, and multiplying her productions beyond all power of thought.

But here Art, the handmaid of Nature, must be called in to her assistance; and care, and skill, and study are required to preserve, cultivate, and display those gifts to advantage, without which they are liable to perish, and

without which half their beauty and excellence are lost or unseen.

To the man of leisure and retirement,
horticulture is a pursuit at once rational and
amusing; it unites the ' utile dulci,' and
gives health and recreation alike to the body
and the mind; the spade, the hoe, and the
rake, even in the hands of a gentleman,
degrade not, when used for such beneficial
ends.

To the invalid and valetudinarian, as well
as to the sufferer from mental distress and
agony, it presents a solace and a balm that at
times seem to abate pain, and give to distress
the languid smile of pleasure. Females, both
young and old, derive the highest gratification
from the flower-garden in particular; and the
more refined the taste, the more exquisite the
gratification. The vernal sun, in the morn-
ings of April and May, emits rays which

kindle pleasure in the breast of the youthful
maiden, who rises early, perambulates the
garden, and feasts the eye and sense upon
the varied beauty and refreshing fragrance of
flowers, so enchantingly displayed in the gay
parterre of art and nature.   This early exer-
cise paints the rose of health upon her cheek,
and the innocency of the recreation imparts
the odour and the purity of the lily to her
mind : this is a pleasure unknown to those
who live in crowded cities, and listless lie in
bed till noon.

> ' Sweet is the breath of Morn, her rising sweet,
>   With charm of earliest birds; pleasant the Sun,
>   When first on this delightful land he spreads
>   His orient beams, on herb, tree, fruit, and flower,
>   Glitt'ring with dew.'   MILTON.

The garden is likewise the private sanctuary
of the pious man's devotions, and the scene
of his meditations : the flower is to him at
once a text and a sermon, which in the morn-

ing may be considered the emblem of youth,
and beauty, and at night, either the drooping
picture of decline, or the withered, lifeless
victim of dissolution. The poet and the
painter are both indebted to the flower-garden. What simple, yet what elegant and
striking metaphors, similes, and apostrophes,
has not the poet drawn from the Rose, the
Tulip, and the Lily! From these, too, the
painter first learns his expression of nature,
and studies the art of colouring, with which
he afterwards gives seeming life and anima-
tion to the more sublime subjects of his pencil.

' I have neither the Scholar's melancholy, which is emulation;
nor the Musician's, which is fantastical; nor the Courtier's, which
is proud; nor the Soldier's, which is ambition; nor the Lawyer's,
which is politic; nor the Lady's, which is nice; nor the Lover's,
which is all these.'   SHAKSPEARE.

It is true that the fancies and tastes of men
are various and singular. Natural history, in
its several divisions and parts, engages the

study and attention of many.. One is fond of plants; another of shells and minerals; another of birds and beasts; another of insects.. The arts also furnish objects of pursuit and amusement. One is a collector of old paintings; another of old coins and medals; another of ancient arms and armour; another of vases and old china; another of rare and curious books and manuscripts; another of old fiddles and other musical instruments: some covet jewels and precious stones; but all, with very rare exceptions, seem to fix their fancy upon the precious metals—gold and silver; and the reason is, 'omne auro venale,' the alchymist's search after the philosopher's stone having been long given up as altogether hopeless.

> 'When gold becomes their object,'
> Men will break their sleep with thought, their brains
> With care, their bones with industry.—What'
> Can it not do, and undo?'   SHAKSPEARE.

Antiquated maids and childless matrons not unfrequently bestow their affections upon dogs, cats, and birds. Bantams, pigeons, and canary-birds have their particular fanciers; and many are the strange fancies besides. Professors of many of the above-recited pursuits are styled Antiquaries, Virtuosi, Connoisseurs, Amateurs, Dilettanti, Fanciers, &c. &c.; and the epithets, sometimes not inaptly applied to them, are learned, curious, skilful, clever—crack-brained, foolish, mad, &c. &c.; and many men are such eccentrics and latitudinists, that, in the course of their lives, they will embrace the whole circle of fancies, and frequently become the dupes ten times over of the knaves, quacks, and varlets of pretended science in each pursuit. Every age, it is true, has its hobby or ruling passion of some sort or other, which varies with our years, as we pass from childhood to youth, from youth to manhood, and from manhood to old age; and those hobbies or recreations, call them which you will, are the pleasantest and best which leave no painful recollections behind them. Yet some aged and self-disappointed philosopher, or peevish moralist, to whom such pursuits no longer present either novelty or gratification, will tell you that the sum of them all is folly, the substance a time-amusing shadow, and the end disappointment and ' vexation of spirit;' but we find that few or none are willing to listen to him, however famed for his wisdom and experience, whose present preaching and past practice have been at variance with each other.

The nature of man still remains the same, though his mind be ever so much improved by education, or enlightened by the collective wisdom and experience of ages; he is subject to the same appetites and passions, influenced by the same tastes and distates, fond of novelty,

the slave of custom and fashion; pleased with
a plaything one moment, and tired of it the
next: his objects of pursuit are often, too, as
fleeting and transitory as the vain wish which
first gave birth to it; mere phantoms of the
imagination, bubbles of air, which very often
vanish in the pursuit, or perish in the attain-
ment: hence it follows that the same career
is run, and the same beaten track trodden as
before.

To particularize any two or three flowers
in this place might appear invidious, yet I
trust I shall incur no displeasure from my
readers, while I just place before their eyes
the names of a few well-known favourites,
which want not my aid either to extol their
beauty or to speak their praise.

> ' Now, my fairest friend,
> I would I had some flowers o' the spring; Daffodils,
> That come before the swallow dares, and take
> The winds of March with beauty; Violets dim,
> But sweeter than the lids of Juno's eyes,

'Or Cytherea's breath ; pale Primroses,
That die unmarried, ere they can behold
Bright Phœbus in his strength, a malady
Most incident to maids ; bold Oxlips, and
The Crown imperial ; Lilies of all kinds,
The flower-de-lis being one ! O these I lack
To make you garlands of !'

SHAKSPEARE.

Who, that has a garden and a taste for
flowers, would be without the Crocus, the
Snowdrop, the Primrose, the Violet, the
Cyclamen, Hepatica, Hyacinth, Narcissus,
Auricula, Ranunculus, Anemone, Wallflower,
Stock, Pink, Tulip, Carnation, Rose, Iris,
Lily, Lychnis, Lobelia, Delphinium, Verbascum, Rudbeckia, Anthericum, Aconitum, Monarda, Ferraria, Gentiana, Ænothera, Scilla
peruviana, Pæony, Phlox, Hemerocallis, Co-
reopsis, Campanula, China Aster, Hollyhock,
and a multitude of others, each species consisting of many beautiful varieties, both single
and double—not to enumerate any of the fine
flowering shrubs of almost every description?

To proceed to the subject immediately before me, — which, in fact, is nothing more than the attempt to describe the mode of treatment necessary to be pursued in the cultivation of a very small part of the flowers just named.

Before I enter upon it, it may perhaps be expected that I should first state some reason or other why I have been induced to publish the following concise and practical treatise on the culture of these flowers (so I have thought fit to style it), since these flowers and their mode of treatment are described more or less in almost every book on gardening. If I should attempt to give any such reason, most likely it would appear to many neither sufficiently weighty nor satisfactory, inasmuch as it would neither prove the necessity of any such publication, nor show that I, from my habits of life, not being professionally a gardener, am competent to the task which I have professed to undertake: however, with all due deference, I beg to state, that I have no where been able to meet with that account of those flowers, and their management, which I from my own knowledge and experience would be induced to adopt and follow, as a manual or directory—because the directions given are too vague, general, and defective, to be reduced to practice; in many cases, also, I have found them quite contrary to the nature and habits of the plants they profess to treat of. Besides, the work of any writer on the flower-garden, whose inmates are now almost without number, however skilful and experienced he might be, if he were to attempt to give plain, clear, and practical directions for the culture of each flower separately, that is worthy of his notice, would be both too expensive to be obtained generally, as well as

too voluminous and unwieldy for general or
every-day use; and in truth, this objection
applies to most of the books already published
on the subject.

Whatever inclination I might have felt to
communicate at all times the result of my
experience to others, I have been greatly
encouraged in the present instance by the
repeated solicitations of several admirers as
well as growers of flowers, to whom I had
already presented in writing, with no small
trouble and inconvenience, the substance of
the remarks contained herein, to print and
publish some short treatise or other on the
Carnation in particular, accompanied with a
catalogue of those flowers which I was in the
habit of growing.

What gave rise in the first instance to
these solicitations was no doubt the fine,
healthy appearance of the plants in my col-

lection, and the uncommonly rich and beautiful blossoms which they have produced the
last two or three years; which circumstance
also served to convince me that the compost
which I had made use of was good, and the
treatment they had received was proper; and
that in publishing the said Treatise and Catalogue, I might render an acceptable service
to the cultivators of flowers in general; the
latter, to direct the young and inexperienced
florist in his choice of good flowers ; and the
former, to assist him in the proper cultivation
of them.

With what clearness and precision I have
executed the same, within the narrow compass prescribed, I leave to the candid and
impartial reader to judge, whose approbation
and patronage I am anxious to obtain.

To say that the design was at last hastily
formed, and as hastily executed, without the

aid of books on the subject to refer to, the whole having been written, printed, and published in the course of a few weeks, under many disadvantages, allowing neither much time for revision nor correction, will perhaps afford but a poor apology for any defects that may appear.

CONTENTS.

TREATISE

ON THE

GROWTH AND MANAGEMENT

OF THE

CARNATION.

ITS NAME AND DISTINCTIONS.

OF all the flowers that adorn the garden, whether
they charm the eye by their beauty, or regale the
sense of smelling by their fragrance, the Carnation
may be justly said to hold the first rank.

> PERDITA. The fairest flowers o' the season
> Are our Carnations, and streaked Gillyflowers,
> Which some call Nature's bastards: of that kind
> Our rustic garden's barren; and I care not
> To get slips of them.
> POLIXINES.   Wherefore, gentle maiden,
> Do you neglect them ?
> > *Shakspeare's Winter's Tale, Act IV.*

The stateliness of its growth, the brilliancy and
diversity of its colours, and the sweetness of its per-

B

fume, never fail to attract our regard and admiration. The Tulip, though styled the Queen of the Garden, cannot boast of more admirers: they may with propriety be considered the two master-pieces of nature; and, though rival beauties, may be said to share the sovereignty of the garden equally between them. Yet it must be admitted that the Carnation, independent of its fragrance, has this advantage over its rival, that it continues longer in bloom; and that when planted in pots, it can be removed to decorate the greenhouse, the conservatory, or the drawing-room.

The Carnation as well as the Pink are said to have been introduced first into England from Italy, and have derived their names in the English language from their colour—Pink, Carnation, or flesh-colour. The Carnation was also, as well as the Clove, styled by the old English florists, Clove-Gilliflower, from its blooming in July. They both belong to the same class and genus, and are known to the ancient botanists under the name of Caryophyllum, or Walnut Leaf, Folium Nucis; but why, is uncertain.

The Carnation is also called Coronarium, from its having been used in chaplets and garlands for the head : Linnæus has now given it the more appropriate appellation of Dianthus, Flos nobilis, fine or superior flower; and Dianthus Caryophyllus, in the modern acceptation of the word, denotes the.Clove only. The Carnation is usually divided into three classes, namely, Flake, Bizarre, and Picotée.

Flake is a term too well known and understood to require any explanation or definition here; Bizarre, the second, is an epithet or adjective borrowed from the French, implying whimsical or fantastical; hence Bizarre, applied to a Carnation, means that it contains a whimsical or fantastical mixture of colours of not less than three distinct shades: Picotée is likewise a French word, an adjective feminine, and signifies pricked or spotted; hence ' la Carnation picotée,' means the spotted Carnation.

The English florist is almost inclined to treat the Picotée as a distinct species like the Pink, and though he has preserved the right mode of spelling the word, he gives it an English pronunciation. To take up the time of the reader in giving a minute description of all the parts of this flower in the technical language of a botanist, is neither necessary nor required here: I will therefore simply describe what are considered the properties of a good flower among florists.

The two first classes are further distinguished by their various colours; as scarlet flake, pink flake, purple flake, scarlet bizarre, crimson bizarre, purple bizarre; the Picotée is distinguished by the colour of its spots.

THE DESCRIPTION OF A FINE CARNATION.

THE excellency of a Carnation is judged and estimated by the brightness and distinctness of its various tints and hues, and by the formation or construction of the flower-leaves or petals : the ground colour should be of a clear white, as in Walker's British Beauty and Sharpe's Defiance, and the flakes or stripes must run longitudinally through the leaves, as in Fletcher's Duchess of Devonshire and

Harley's Enchanter, not breaking off abruptly, as in Belcher's Lady Spenser. ' In a perfect flower, or one that approaches nearest to perfection, every leaf should be striped according to its class, whether flake or bizarre : plain or self-coloured leaves are accounted a great defect. The calix or cup, after the petals are unfolded, must remain entire and unburst, and the large external petals or guard leaves must be without crack or blemish; and the diameter of a show-flower should never be less than three inches. It is also considered a great defect when the corolla is overcharged with petals, as in Reynolds's King and Young's Mount Ætna, for the blossom in expanding generally bursts the cup; and it is no less so when it contains too few, as is the case with Crump's Rodney, Wood's Comet, and Anne's Prince of Wales, though possessing the most brilliant and distinct colours. It is unnecessary, perhaps, to state here that those flowers which are thin of leaves produce the most seed, on which account they are valuable.

The flower must be sufficiently double to form a

kind of crown in the centre, as in Davey's Tower of
Babel and James's Lord Craven, the petals rising
one above another in regular order; the guard leaves
in particular should be broad and long, and of a
stout texture, to support the rest, like those of Humphrey's Duke of Clarence, the edges of which must
not be indented or fringed, as unluckily is the case
with Honey's Princess Charlotte, but plain and circular, like the leaves of a Provins Rose. A flower,
whose corolla or pod is long, generally shoots forth
the finest flower, and occasions the least trouble
in attending it. The flower or foot stalk must be
strong, straight, and elastic, to support the blossoms
firmly and gracefully, notwithstanding the stick
which is applied to sustain it; the height of the
stalk varies from 2 ft. 6 in. to 4 ft. 6 in. according to
the habit of their growth.

The value of a flower is also greatly enhanced,
when it exhales a sweet and fragrant perfume, as is
the case with Robinson's Britannia, Weltje's Sir
Edward Pellew, Broadbent's Victorious, Bates's
Wellington, &c. All Carnations possess this qua-

lity, but in very different degrees; in some it is scarcely perceptible, while in others it is strikingly powerful. Odour seems to prevail most in strongly bizarred scarlets, where there is a frequent recurrence of the clove stripe in the petals. The preference which one class of flowers, at times, is said to obtain over another, depends entirely on the taste and fancy of the person who gives that preference. The scarlet bizarre is a favourite with one, the crimson with another, the purple flake with another, and so on in like manner with the rest. There can be no certain or fixed rule why one is to be adjudged in this respect superior to another, where taste is the only criterion to go by. A flower possessed of all the properties called for by the rules and regulations laid down in the Societies, where they are exhibited for prizes, is seldom or never met with. Art is called in to the assistance of nature, and the skilful hand of the florist dexterously extracts the self-coloured and defective and over-crowded leaves, and sometimes even will insert others, and arranges and adjusts the whole with surprising nicety.

One Christopher Nunn, of Enfield, Middlesex, a noted florist in his day, was eminent for his skill and dexterity in dressing Pinks and Carnations for prize exhibitions; some will even tell you, that Kit was the father of the art.   Upon such occasions he had as many applications to dress flowers, as he had to dress wigs; for he was a barber and friseur by trade, and withal a good-natured, facetious, prating barber, and could both shave and lay a Carnation with the greatest nicety.   The novices of that day, who, being unacquainted with his secret art, trusted to Dame Nature to open, expand, and perfect their flowers, were no match for Nunez: for he began where she left off, and perfected what she had left imperfect.—His arrangement and disposition of the petals were admirable, and astonished those novices. Kit's art of dressing is still an enviable art, and attainable only by few.

Kit, as a florist, possessed other merit besides this: he could mix and temper soils with the same skill as he did his pomatum; he was a great experimentalist and compounder of manures; it was all

the same to him, whether he snuffed up the odour
of roses, or the less inviting fragrance of animal
ordure; it was he that first applied sugar-bakers'
scum as a surface dressing to flowers, having witnessed its surprising effect upon the land of a neighbour of his, a sugar-refiner from Goodman's Fields;
and he also had the credit of persuading and con-
vincing Sir Somebody Tressilian or Trevannian, a
Cornish Baronet, that old rags and old wigs, which
contained so much grease and human fat, were a
much warmer and richer manure for his land, than
the oily carcasses of his pilchards; and it is further
said, that Kit, as agent or factor, in one week bought
up more than two thousand wigs in the neighbourhood of that celebrated mart Rosemary Lane, which
were sent down to try the experiment. Be not im-
patient, courteous reader, to get rid of poor Nunn;
remember he was a brother florist, and belonged to
the fancy—wait till you learn the result of one of
his own experiments, and take this moral with it,
though there be no fable here:—' Other men's mis-
haps should make us wary.'

In the early stage of his fancy, Kit, upon
mature reflection, once concluded, that neat and
genuine horse-dung, divested of all extraneous straw,
must be better than much straw and little dung, as
are usually put together. The resolution once taken,
he hastened to the shop of a neighbouring black-
smith, and agreed for all the droppings that the
horses, which came to be shod, should make in a
twelvemonth, with all the parings of the hoof to
boot. He amassed above two loads of this dung,
and after it had become rotten, he mixed it up with
the mould for his flowers in every way; he made
use of it for Pinks and Carnations, both in pots and
in beds. His expectations for a fine bloom that
summer were raised to the highest pitch, and yet
ended in disappointment: his plants, towards Midsummer, began to look yellowish and sickly, and
turn cankery about the roots; his bloom, too, was
very indifferent; and what could be the cause?
His loam, he was sure, was sweet and good, and his
dung was nothing but dung. He layered the plants:
the layers also turned sickly, and several of them

perished. Kit's lamentations about his flowers were loud and incessant; they were heard in all the villages around him—he repeated them to his customers at home and abroad—and the cause—he could not divine the cause.

It was well for him that all this happened before Mr. Pitt, prime minister of state, had laid a sumptuary tax on heads that wore hair powder; had these two evils occurred at the same time, they must have broken poor Nunn's heart. But to cut the tale short, in the same way that the said tax cut off the pig-tails of many of his customers afterwards, Kit was not aware, till he had been informed by some chemist, naturalist, or botanist, that the hobnails, the filings, the flakes, and the bits of iron, that had been swept up and mixed with the dung, had been the cause of all the mischief, and which had produced that ' salsa rubigo,' rust and canker, which had corrupted and poisoned the juices of the plants, and nearly destroyed the whole. He never after could endure the sight of a rusty nail in his compost. So much for poor Christopher Nunn!

MODE OF DRESSING A FLOWER.

I HARDLY dare attempt to draw an outline even of this sublime art of dressing a flower, because I have neither studied nor practised it myself; and therefore not being entitled to a diploma, I must neither assume the title nor degree of A.M., that is, Artis Magister, by which alone I might be held qualified to teach it, but must be content to be considered only as a pretender and quack upon this abstruse point. However, let us see what sort of a handle I shall make of it. In the first place, then, provide yourselves with proper instruments, namely, a pair of brass or ivory etui, commonly called tweezers, and a small ivory bodkin.

As soon as the guard-leaves drop, clap a card on, and with your bodkin, from time to time, assist the petals in falling into their places; then fix a glass cap over the blossom, to bleach the white, and to enable the leaves, by the warmth, to expand freely; shade the glass, when the sun is out, with a cabbage leaf or bit of canvas; take the glass off for an hour or two in the evening to expose the blossom to the air, lest the colours become faint by too much confinement, and lose their lustre.

Not to spin this subject out too fine, we will suppose that to-morrow the grand exhibition takes place, the show-day for honour and prizes; and that you have already marched and countermarched from one end of the stage or garden to the other, times out of number, and that you have examined and re-examined all the blooms over and over, and that you have at length, towards evening, fixed upon and cut the seven or twelve flowers, as the number may be, which are to grace the pan, and contend for the prize.

Dissolve a little nitre or saltpetre in the water, before you put your flowers in it; this will help to stiffen the leaves. After they have been in water a couple of hours, take your etui, and pull the guard-leaves quite round and circular; then place the second, third, and fourth tier of petals in an imbricated form, that is, like slates upon a roof, or scales upon a fish,—a leaf covering each division of the

leaves in each row or tier, till they are all arranged
in a convex form, like the outside of a dome or
cupola; place the bizarred and finely-striped leaves
in full sight, pluck out all white or self-coloured,
all pouncy and superfluous dull leaves; and those
that will not lie, whirl with your bodkin into the
crown of the flower; let the blooms be set in the
cellar, or coolest part of the house, all night over a
tub of water; mind that the clefts or fissures down
the sides of the pod do not reach below the bottom
external cup, and that the guard-leaves stand firm
and support themselves without the card. A practical lesson, after all, upon the flower is worth a
dozen theoretical upon paper: learn this art by
practice, and practise to learn.

The show-day is an anxious day with a young
florist: he is full of hopes and fears, and it is not
less so with an old one, for ' the battle is not always
to the strong, nor the race to the swift;' for there
are instances without number where many an old
experienced, good florist has been beat, and obliged
to return home, alas! without either silver cup, silver

spoons, punch-ladle, copper kettle, or set of china, to the no small disappointment of a prize-expecting ' *cara sposa*' at home, who not unfrequently repays his ill-luck and empty-handedness.with a good sharp lecture upon his neglect and want of management.

Nay, nay, blush not, you heroes of Middlesex, nor you doughty yeomen of Lancashire, Yorkshire, or other county; for if a wife has no right to tell a. husband of his faults, who has?

———————

SITUATION, SOILS, &c.

To produce blossoms in any degree answering the description contained in the last chapter, it is requisite, in the first place, that the plants should be judiciously selected, and also that they should be in good health and vigour. How to effect the latter is at all times the chief aim and study of the experienced florist.

An open and airy situation is the most proper for the Carnation, as being most congenial to its growth

in all its stages. The florists in the immediate vicinity of the metropolis certainly labour under great
disadvantages in this particular, from the atmosphere
being almost always charged with clouds of unwhole-
some smoke, ascending from such an infinity of
chimneys.

The Carnation is found to thrive best in a rich
loamy soil of rather a sandy texture; and unless
some pains be taken to procure such a soil, the florist
can have no right to entertain any great hopes of
success in the cultivation of it; the dissertation on
which, with the account of the different manures
recommended, and which presents itself next to my
consideration, may perhaps appear tedious and too
minute to many, but certainly it is of the greatest
importance to every gardener as well as florist to
understand something of the nature and composition
of the soils most congenial to the plants he has to
cultivate: this is a point, in my opinion, which can
neither be too minutely explained, nor too strongly
inculcated.

PRIMITIVE SOILS.

EARTH, in regard to its different qualities, is divided into four sorts of native or primitive soils, viz. argillaceous or loamy, calcareous or chalky, siliceous or sandy, heathy and boggy or peaty, and these are further distinguished according to their nature, whether stiff or light, as clayey, gravelly, marly, &c.

Maiden or vegetable mould, which is formed by the decay of all vegetable and animal substances, forms the superficial stratum of all soils, and is considered the most fertile of all. The grand art in gardening is to know when there is deficiency or redundancy of any of those primitive soils in the mould you are going to make use of, and to be able to mix and regulate it, so as to suit the nature and wants of the tree, shrub, or plant you intend to set in it.

' There are many people who, from want of
' thought or observation, foolishly imagine, that be-
' cause a plant is set in mould it must thrive in it,
' exposed in all weathers—wet or dry, hot or cold;

' whether it be tender or hardy, indigenous or exotic;
' whether it be a native of the mountains or an off-
' spring of the valleys; never considering that dif-
' ferent plants require different soils or earths, as well
' as different aspects and climates.   Some require
' strong soils, others light; some like to bask in the
' sun, others thrive best in the shade; some will stand
' any flood of rain, while others again require moisture
' only occasionally; from which it is pretty evident
' that one general system of culture for every plant
' can be neither right nor proper.   To mix, temper,
' and harmonize different soils, so as to form one
' suitable to each plant, to know its peculiar situation
' and proper treatment, its best mode of propagation,
' &c., is what shows and distinguishes the skilful
' and experienced gardener.' — *Emmerton on the
Auricula.*

DIRECTIONS IN THE CHOICE OF YOUR LOAM.

I HERE recommend to all who have the means or
opportunity of doing it, to lay up a sufficient stock

of rich loam or maiden earth to serve them two or three years, which, by being turned occasionally, will become pulverised and fit for use at all times and for all purposes. What you obtain from any waste or common, should consist, in the language of a labouring man, of the top spit and crumbs only, to be piled up with the turf downwards. The common test whereby to judge of a rich soil is, that when fresh dug up it shall emit a pleasant smell, and not stick to the fingers in handling, but when compressed and rubbed between the thumb and fingers, will feel soft and oily. Another opinion of its goodness may also be formed this way; that is, where you see trees grow freely, or rich and luxuriant crops of corn or grass appear, you may take it for granted that the soil they grow in is good. That in which you perceive veins of rust or oxide of iron, called by farmers till or fox-bent, ought to be avoided, or at least it ought not to be used till after it has lain some time, been repeatedly turned, and exposed to all the action of the weather—rain, sun, and air.

After having made choice of your soil, the next

inquiry is, how it may be improved, and made to contribute in a higher degree to vegetation.

I shall now proceed to describe the process which
I have used for its amelioration, and state the different component parts or ingredients which I have
mixed and put together as a *compost* for Carnations,
the same which I have used with success for some
years, and which I now beg to recommend to my
brother florists for trial.

COMPOST, MODE OF PREPARING IT, &c.

In putting the different soils together for compost,
particular care must be taken to make it of such
consistency, that, when in pots, the water shall neither
pass through it too rapidly, nor lodge too long in it;
both are hurtful. If the loam be of a strong, stiff
nature, it will require a greater portion of sand to be
added; if light, it will require less. You will therefore, in the first instance, be guided by the nature

and quality of your loam or mould: this I hold extremely essential to be attended to.

Kirwan, in his Treatise on Manures, expressly states, ' That the proportion of each ingredient, and ' the general texture of the soil, must be such, as to ' enable it to admit and retain as much water as is ' necessary to vegetation, and no more.'

The simple earths or soils, it is well known, vary greatly in regard to their retentive powers of preserving moisture. The time that I generally set about mixing the compost is towards the end of the summer, when the melons and cucumbers have done bearing, whose beds furnish me with the dung proper for my purpose.

Requiring a large quantity of mould, for I mostly bloom about 500 pots of Carnations, I take in the following ratios :

    1 Load of fresh yellow loam,

    ½ Ditto of common black earth or garden mould,

    2 Ditto of rotten horse-dung,

    4 Large barrows of coarse sand from some

wash or pond by the high road side, or
dry road grit in lieu thereof, laid up to
dry, and run through a sieve.

Note 1. The loam in my neighbourhood being
mostly of a stiff quality, requires a large
portion of sand to bring it to a proper
consistency, to enable the water to pass
through in any moderate time.

„   2. Rotten dung from mushroom beds ought
not to be used in this compost, on account
of the fungous fibres.

For an abridged quantity, say—

5 Barrows of loam, or maiden earth,

8 or 9 Ditto of horse-dung, from the frames,

1 Ditto of coarse sand, or more, according to
the nature of the loam.

Let these be mixed and thrown together in a heap
or ridge, and turned two or three times in the
winter, particularly in frosty weather, that it may be
well incorporated.

On a dry day towards the end of November, I
take a barrow of fresh lime, which, as soon as it is
slacked, I strew it over while hot in turning the

heap; this accelerates the rotting of the fibrous particles in the loam, lightens the soil, and destroys the grubs, worms, and slugs. Lime is too well known as a manure to say anything further in its praise here.

APPLICATION OF SALT AS A MANURE.

If there has been much rain during the winter, so that the strength of the compost is reduced, and the salts washed from it, I take about 7 lbs. of damaged salt, and add them to it, either dissolved in water, or strewed over with the hand. This, from an experience of three years, I have found to be attended with the most beneficial effect upon the future health and vigour of the plants.

During very heavy rains, many florists cover their compost with tarpaulin or double mats, to prevent the nutritious particles from being washed out; this is also an excellent precaution.

If any objection be started, that the quantity of

dung is too great in proportion to that of the loam, I answer, that such an objection might be well-founded, if the compost were to be used immediately on its being mixed together; but as it has to lie six months before it is used, I am decidedly of opinion that the quantity is not more than is necessary in order to insure a luxuriant growth and a generous bloom.

It is, moreover, indispensably necessary, that the compost should lie that time; that the different ingredients may be properly incorporated one with another; that the loam may be well pulverized, and the whole duly prepared and sweetened by frequent turning; and that the carbonaceous principle of matter in the dung, according to Hassenfraz, may, through the medium of the rains, like a leaven, extend to and pervade the whole mass, so as to render it fit, wholesome, and nutritious food for the plants it has to sustain.

CONSTITUENT PRINCIPLES OF PLANTS.

IT may perhaps not be thought improper in this place to state, that all plants, by chemical analysis, are found to consist of particles of calcareous earth, oil, water, and air, with a portion of iron.

CHARACTERISTICS OF A BAD AND GOOD FLORIST, &c.

THE gentleman or lady's gardener, who has no other motive to incite him, beyond that of performing what he is ordered to do, will imagine all this vast preparation of soils, all this extraordinary commixtion, a very unnecessary and useless trouble, and will be disposed to slight and neglect it. In fact, I have nowhere seen flowers so ill-treated and mismanaged (with few exceptions) as in the gardens of the nobility and gentry, even when there has been a collection of fine flowers; I allude not to Carnations

C

and Pinks only, but to flowers generally. Yet, on the other hand, there is a strong apology to be offered for this neglect in the gardener, as far as it regards Carnations and Pinks, for I have mostly noticed them to be of the worst and most common description, such as I would not give a place to in my garden. To cultivate a bad flower, which has neither beauty nor hardly any smell, is attended with the same trouble as there is in cultivating a good one; and, in the present greatly improved state of both, there is no difficulty to select good ones.

But the thorough-bred florist, who derives pleasure from the pursuit, and who has always the flower-fever strong upon him; who has rivals to contend with; who is incited by the love of fame, and the hope of winning the first splendid prize at some exhibition; who will walk fifty miles to catch a glimpse of some new celebrated flower, and who, if it meets his fancy, will sooner pawn the coat from off his back, than not obtain it; who will leave his warm and comfortable bed at midnight, to rise and destroy the cursed earwigs, that shall dare to attack his favourite blossom; will begrudge no labour, and neglect no pains, to perform this part well, on which he knows his chance of success principally depends. With the latter, especially if he be young in the fancy, my only fear is, lest he over-do his part. To such a one, if you give a receipt for any particular composition, and recommend one peck of soot, most probably he will put two—if two pounds of salt, he will put four—if three pails of blood, he will put six—if four barrows of sugar-baker's scum, he will put eight—and so on.

REMOVING OF THE PLANTS INTO LARGE POTS TO BLOOM.

In our variable climate, the first week in April is the safest and best time to perform this: the pots generally made use of for this purpose, are those of twelve or sixteen to a cast.

A twelve-sized pot will contain three or four plants, according to their habit of growth—a six-

teen, two or three, according to the same rule. Be
careful to put two or three large bits of tile at the
bottom, or the hollow part of a large oyster-shell,
resting upon a tile, to preserve a secure drainage for
the water. Stagnant water, whether in pots or in
the open fields, is alike prejudicial to all plants,
except aquatics.

The pots to be filled three parts full with compost, in its rough or coarse state from the heap,
using fine or sifted mould only at the top, around
the roots of the plants, which must not be planted
deeper than they were before.

The mould to be well shaken down, to prevent its
settling after. The coarse parts, or riddlings, that
would not pass through the sieve, may also be put
at the bottom, filling each pot about three inches
deep with them.

At this season of the year, when they want water,
let it be given in the morning, rather than in the
evening, till about the middle of May, on account of
the frosts which will often recur at that time. When
the plants begin to spindle, or shoot up for bloom,

they require to be supported by sticks, about four feet in length; some of tall growth, as Humphrey's Clarence, Snook's Defiance, Fulbrook's Grenadier, Wood's Ambassador, &c., require sticks five feet long.

THE APHIS, OR GREEN FLY.

IN some seasons, these Aphides, or flies, appear in astonishing numbers, as was the case last summer, and attack the Rose and Carnation in particular. They congregate in countless swarms round the stems and on the foliage of both, and adhere closely to the bud of the Rose and the pod of the Carnation, to the great injury of the health of both.

They should be brushed off from the Carnation with a soft brush repeatedly; but if this is found inefficient to dislodge and disperse them, take some pungent Scotch snuff and scatter over them, two or three times, when the plants are moist, or covered with dew. A weak infusion of tobacco in water may be applied with a soft brush with effect, and without

injury.   A weak infusion of lime-water and sulphur
may also be used in a clarified state.

THE EAR-WIG.

OF all the enemies that the Carnation has to encounter, the ear-wig is the most troublesome and
destructive.   It attacks that part of the flower which
is called the nectarium, and eats the petals through
just at their root; if it be not sufficiently open to
admit its descent down the corolla, it will eat its way
to it through the outside of the calix.

There is no entire preventive, but the most effectual method is, to support your stage upon legs,
placed in cast-iron pans, about six inches deep, filled
with water.   Bean-stalks, cut into lengths of six or
eight inches, may be set as traps round the stage,
and close to the stems of the flower, which should be
examined every morning at least, and the ear-wigs
blown out into a bottle of water.

Bowls of tobacco-pipes, or the claws of lobsters,

may be placed for the same purpose on the tops of the sticks; but, use what precautions you will, you cannot entirely prevent their ravages.

An experienced florist once informed me that he usually fixed a small bit of sponge, or cotton dipped in sweet oil, to the stick that supports the stem; he assured me that he had every reason to be satisfied with this experiment, and that it proved an effectual barrier to the passage of the ear-wig and other insects.

Nr. Nicol, in his ' Gardener's Calendar,' recommends a pencil or small brush to be dipped in oil, and drawn round the pot, near the bottom, when they are in flower, every two or three days, to prevent the ear-wigs and snails from climbing up and doing any injury. Sweet-oil, or rather linseed-oil as the cheapest, may be used in this way, I have no doubt, with a good effect; for sweet-oil, if it comes in contact with the bodies of most insects, will occasion their almost immediate death.

THE GRUB.

THERE is another foe which you must guard against,
a grub, about an inch long, of the caterpillar tribe,
of a green, olive, or brown colour, according to the
food it feeds on : it will ascend the stalk during the
night, and consume part of the petals, eating holes
in the pod, and then descend, and bury itself during
the day, just under the surface of the mould, often
near the foot of the stem; and so will continue to
renew its attack night after night.   When the blossom is in a dying state, it will often secrete itself in
the seed-vessel, and devour the whole interior of that
and every other on the stem, if not discovered.

THE WIRE-WORM.

THE wire-worm, of a yellowish cast, with a black
head, and nearly an inch in length when full grown,
is another destructive enemy to the Carnation and

Pink. As it works below the surface of the ground, it is not easily detected; nothing, in fact, but the dead or dying state of the plant points out its retreat. It attacks the stem just at the root, and will perforate it through and through. It is introduced into gardens, for the most part, with the fresh loam, in the turning of which the eye should always be on the look-out for this pernicious insect, which, when met with, never, I believe, escapes destruction.

I met with two a few days ago, and tried what effect a little quick lime had upon them. I scattered a little over them, but it seemed to make no other impression than to induce them to move from it with more speed than they are generally accustomed to do. I brought them back to it again, and kept them there for a couple of minutes; but they were still able to crawl from it, apparently not much hurt by it, and they effected their retreat to a heap of mould hard by. The only sure way to deal with them, is, ' to catch them and kill them.'

I am very little acquainted with the natural history of this destructive insect, which breeds with as-

tonishing rapidity : it deposits its eggs in the ground
like the slug, without any particular precaution; in
turning over lately some horse-dung, which had lain
in the corner of a kitchen-garden two or three years,
I discovered and picked out several of these eggs,
which were of various sizes, from a pin's head to that
of a small sweet-scented pea just beginning to sprout.
I took one of the largest of these bladdery-formed
substances, and with a gentle pressure of the finger
and thumb, forced through a small aperture at the
top of the neck five of these insects, one after another,
completely formed, and able to crawl about. The
rest, which were in a less forward state, were collected
and put into a saucer, and being exposed to the sun
were soon dried up, the external membrane or bladder
only remaining.

TOP DRESSING IN JUNE.

As frequent watering of the plants in pots, in dry
and hot seasons, must tend to exhaust the vegetative

powers of the compost, and weaken its strength, I generally, about the beginning or middle of June, top-dress, with about half an inch of rotten horse-dung passed through a sieve, which I find materially to assist the plants, and promote the growth of the layers, on which depends the preservation of your collection. Many top-dress with some of the hotter manures of night-soil, sugar-baker's scum, &c., but, in my opinion, that is not necessary for Carnations, and is attended with danger; for, if they are not reduced to a perfect mould, they will corrode and burn the plants.

An immoderate use of strong manures to most plants, is like the immoderate use of hot spirituous liquors to the human frame; they force and excite for a time, only to weaken and destroy.

HOT MANURES, AND THE APPLICATION OF THEM.

STRONG compost, in which the chief ingredients are sugar-baker's scum, soap-boiler's waste, night-soil, the dung of pigeons and poultry in general, of deer and sheep, blood, soot, lime, gypsum, &c. &c. should, in my humble opinion, be used only in surface or top-dressing of flowers; as is the case when applied to land, unless you are disposed to wait two or three years, till they have lost much of their strength, and are reduced nearly to mould; they may then be used as simple ingredients along with loam.

A few short observations respecting two or three of which, may, perhaps, not prove unacceptable in this place.

Blood, as a manure, is considered the strongest and most lasting of all, and, when mixed up with mould as a compost, is not fit for use under two complete years. The same is the case with night-soil, sugar-baker's scum, pigeon-dung, &c. Soot is of that hot, caustic nature, that it ought always to be used with caution, and in small quantities. The dung of sheep I consider the most fertilizing to all grasses, and I recommend it as an excellent ingredient in all composts for Pinks, Carnations, and Auriculas; because, in all pastures and meadows, where any considerable flock of sheep has been grazing any length of time, so as to leave behind a tolerable dressing of dung, after their removal, you will perceive the grass to shoot up freely, and to assume a rich verdure and healthy appearance; not rank and coarse, yet vigorous and elastic, such as the florist would wish to see his Pinks and Carnations assume, previous to their coming into bloom. This dung, the principal component parts of which are nearly all soluble in water, will not be fit for use till it has been incorporated with the mould a twelvemonth.

· The ingenious florist has frequent recourse to those strong manures, and uses them in various ways. Some he incorporates with his compost, in which he grows his plants—some he uses separately and unmixed, for surface-dressing—others he infuses in water, and applies in a liquid state—all this he does from an almost universally received opinion, that they will increase and heighten the colours of his flowers, and give them a brilliancy, which he supposes they never could attain without them.

Plants that live all the year round in pots, parti-

cularly exotics, must, no doubt, be benefited by this
surface-dressing, with the strong manures, which
should be applied a few weeks before they flower ; as
Geraniums, Camelias, Orange-trees, &c.

Towards the end of February, I generally apply
a top-dressing, of about half an inch thick, to the
Double Primrose, Polyanthus, and Auricula, that
are in pots, having first removed the mould at the
top, whose place it has to supply, without injury to
the fibres ; the vegetative and nutritious properties
of which, by watering, long confinement in the frame,
and seclusion from the open air, must be greatly de-
teriorated, if not rendered sour, acrid, and unwhole-
some.

The beneficial effect of such dressing is fully ap-
parent. You need only try the experiment on two
pots, and then compare them with two others, that
you have not meddled with, to be convinced of its
utility.

The improved health and vigour of the plants
will be visible, from their improved verdure and
strength ; their blossoms will be larger and finer, and

the texture of the petals firmer and stronger; their
state and condition will be such as to extort from the
enraptured florist, the following emphatical expression of delight :—

'Here's beauty! Here's cloth, colour, and gold for you!'

An expression which once I heard, with no small
pleasure, acompanied with the most extravagant ges-
ticulation of body.

COMMON GARDEN MANURE.

MANURE for the garden is generally confined to
horse-dung and straw-litter, rotted by frequent turning and working, which excites fermentation, and
hastens its decay; this operation is too frequently
performed in situations where the juices or fluids that
come from it run away and are lost, by which means
the saline and other nutritious qualities are reduced,
and 'the strength and efficacy of the whole greatly
impaired. The carbonaceous principle, likewise,
which is produced by fermentation occasioned by the
decomposition and decay of all vegetable substances,

lying any length of time in a state of putrefaction; as well as by combustion, whether open or hidden; and which forms a very essential part in all vegetative matter, fertilizing the various soils mixed with it, is in a great degree lost to the manure so situated.

The market-gardener will inform you, that one load of horse-dung, sufficiently turned, fermented, and rotted, to enable him to dig it in the ground, is worth three, in point of effect and service, of that which has been used in the forcing of melons and cucumbers.

The best, and in fact the most economical mode of preparing manure, either for the field or garden, and which is now generally practised by all skilful agriculturists as well as horticulturists, is this: I will describe the process upon a small scale, as adapted to the garden.

Take, towards the autumn, two loads of fresh loam or mould from some common waste or upland pasture, spread them eighteen inches thick upon the ground, the spot chosen for which ought to be rather hollow, that is, sloping a little on all sides towards

the centre, in the form of a very shallow bowl; upon
this stratum or bed of mould shoot five or six loads
of horse-dung. This must be turned over and watered if necessary, till it begins to ferment and heat;
this is the first stage of decomposition. The turning
and watering will soon occasion it to decay and rot;
the fermented and strongly impregnated juices pro-
ceeding from the dung, and the ullage occasioned
from time to time by the rains, will all be received
and absorbed in the mould below it, so that none of
the saline particles, which are accounted the grand
fertilizers of the earth, will escape and be lost.

How often emotions of regret, at the folly and ignorance of our English farmers, have been excited in
the breast of the celebrated agriculturist, Arthur
Young, Esq., while riding through the country, in
seeing heaps of manure lying on eminences by the
road sides, and the black, impregnated juices draining from it, and running in waste into the ditches;
which, if they had been preserved in the manner
described, would have served to fertilize their fields;
the residuum being comparatively a corpus mortuum,

deprived of half its virtue, strength, and efficacy.
But to proceed: if you wish to make use of any of
this compost for the choicer vegetables in the kitchen
garden, you have only to mix the whole together,
and apply it in the spring; but if it be intended as
manure to mix with loam for flowering shrubs, pines,
plants, &c., or for flower borders and beds, it will be
requisite to keep it a twelvemonth longer, making
eighteen months in all, before it will be fit for use,
and sufficiently comminuted and rotten to pass
through a coarse sieve. The addition of this fresh
earth to exhausted and worn-out gardens will be attended with much benefit.

In the beginning of March mix and incorporate
the whole together; turn it again in April, and again
in May; then put it together in the form of a ridge,
and let it remain so till Michaelmas. To preserve the
compost from losing its strength, by the powerful
exhalation of its saline properties by the sun in summer, incrustit with mould, or cover it with hurdles of
reeds or with loose litter.

This rule, however, does not apply to such manures as take a longer time to prepare them, before they can be used as compost for delicate flowers. Night-soil requires a constant exposure for two years, to get rid of its strong sulphuric acid; soap-boiler's lye, to neutralize its powerful alkaline salt; sugar-baker's scum, to divest it of its predominant saccharine property; and cow-dung, to correct its crude acetous quality.

Wood-shavings, when rotten and decayed, saw-dust, tan, the bark and small branches of trees in general, lying any length of time, acquire this carbonaceous principle, and make a good ingredient in compost for many plants, the Auricula in particular. It is this coaly property that gives the dark-brown discolouring to water, and of which soot and ashes may be said to contain the very essence.

LEAF-MOULD, ITS USES AND MODE OF PREPARING.

LEAF-MOULD is the finest and most valuable of all the artificial soils, and is used by the skilful gardener

in a variety of ways : with a portion of this, a little
maiden earth, old rotten horse-dung and sand, he
pipes his Pinks, and pipes and lays his Carnations;
in a mixture of this he plants his seedling Auriculas
and young off-sets; there is hardly any plant, however delicate and tender, that will not grow and thrive
in it.

Every one that has the means and opportunity of
doing it, ought, towards the end of October, to collect
the leaves when in a moist state, and put them in a
hole made for that purpose, mixing at the same time
with them a little quick-lime to hasten their decay,
and a small portion of earth.   They may lie in that
state till spring, when they ought to be turned over,
repeating the same about once in six weeks afterwards, till they become quite decayed and pulverized.
If there be not a very great body of leaves together,
by this process they generally become fit for use in
twelve months.

SALT AS A MANURE CONSIDERED.

THE application of salt, and its utility as a manure, are yet imperfectly understood. It is a matter of uncertainty, whether it acts directly as a manure, or only as a kind of spice or seasoning, thereby rendering the soil a more palatable food for plants. Be that as it may, if it acts beneficially in any manner, it ought to be adopted.

The evidence adduced before the late Committee in the House of Commons was of a contradictory nature; yet the preponderance of opinions advanced, and of experiments detailed, was greatly in favour of it. A small pamphlet, published by Mr. Parke on the subject, may be read with much interest.

The main question as it stands at present is, What is the proper quantity to be used on arable or grass lands, and which is the proper time for its application?

I have used it for these three years past in compost for flowers, and shall continue to do so, from a per-

suasion of its beneficial effects. A Scotch gardener,
to whom I related the use of salt as manure, endeavoured to dissuade me from doing it; his opinion,
no doubt, was regulated by the account of the experiment of salt-water (sea-water) given by his coun-
tryman, Walter Nicol. ' Ah, man,' said he, ' it will
destroy all your flowers, root and branch, for nothing
will grow where salt is.' I however still persisted to
use it. Five or six years previous to this, I had a
few favourite Cloves growing in the ground, and was
anxious to protect them from the slugs and snails, by
which their foliage had been much injured; I was
told that salt was an excellent remedy against them;
accordingly I strewed a handful or two of it close to
the roots and over the foliage of the plants, in order,
as I thought, to preserve them from being eaten up by
them; but judge of my surprise—in a few days after,
I observed them to turn yellow and sickly; in fact,
they languished for a while, and died. And such
would have been their fate, if I had put fresh soot,
quick-lime, night-soil, sugar-baker's scum, or any
other hot manure in a green or rank state; from

which circumstance I was not unaware of the effects
of salt injudiciously applied.

CARE OF CARNATIONS—(*continued.*)

PODDING, CARDING, AND WIRING.

CARNATIONS require to be watered freely while the
pods are swelling ; and, in fact, during the whole
time they continue in blossom, they ought to be kept
moist, and never be suffered to flag for want of it.
Most flowers require the same treatment.

At this season it is better to water with the pipe
of the garden-pot, in preference to the rose, and to
pour it upon an oyster-shell, placed on the top of the
flower-pot, to receive and break the force of the
water; this will prevent it from making holes in the
mould, and laying bare the roots. Some sorts seem
to suffer from water, however soft it may be, when
poured all over the layers, in hot weather; the ends
of the grass very often will turn white and sickly, as

if they had been parboiled and scalded. If the
grass appears short and backward for laying, water
once or twice a week, with a weak infusion of horse
or sheep dung, prepared in a tub for that purpose;
this wash will both promote the growth of the layers,
and give a depth and richness of colouring to such
flowers as are apt to come pale and short of it.

As soon as the side-shoots appear, they should be
stripped off, to give strength to the main stem. To
flowers which you intend to exhibit, if a small or
thinnish one, leave only two pods on a stem; to a
large or full one, leave three; there are many exceptions; some require nearly the whole to be left on.

In order to prevent the pods from bursting, or
opening irregularly, a small piece of bass-mat dipt
in water should be carefully tied round the middle of
each pod, but not before it is nearly full-formed; it
will also require easing from time to time, as the pod
continues to increase and grow.

If you perceive the pod inclined to burst on one
side, give ease to it on the other also, by slitting the
cup with a sharp knife, or with a thin bit of ivory,

generally fixed to the end of the etui, made use of for dressing the flower : in a crowded pod it is always best to ease it in time, by cutting the cup in the several indentures or scallops marked at the top; the guard-leaves will then fall in regular order all round.

As soon as the large external petals of the flower or guard-leaves begin to expand, drop, and fall back, a paper collar should be placed round the bottom of the blossom to support it. These collars are made of white thin card paper, in the form of a circle of three or four inches in diameter, with a hole in the centre just large enough to admit the calix or pod, without much compressing, and with a cut extending from the centre to the outside or circumference, like the radius of a circle. On these cards the flower is preserved in shape and form a long time; on these the petals also are finely disposed, and the beauty of the Carnation displayed to great advantage.

To support the blossoms when carded, and to keep them from being blown about by the wind, as well as to sustain the additional weight of the cards, a small thin brass wire, about three inches long,

D

though different lengths are required, in the shape of a common wire skewer, is usually fixed to the stick; one end, which is twisted into the form of a hook or head of a shepherd's crook, is placed round the bottom of the pod; and the other end, which is sharpened, is forced with a pair of wire nippers into the stick. This may be easily effected after a trial or two.

Wire, proper for this use, may be had at any of the wire-shops; there are three or four shops of this description near the Monument, in the city of London, where they manufacture them ready for use, at so much a hundred.

PROTECTION OF THE BLOSSOMS FROM RAIN, &c.

THE moment the Carnations begin to unfold their blossoms, they should be covered from the rain and scorching sun; they should either be covered with small glasses or with paper caps, in the shape of an umbrella, with a tube in the centre, to be fixed on the tops of the sticks. If you would preserve the beauty of a Carnation untarnished, it should not be suffered to have a single drop of rain. Those caps and glasses may be put over the Carnations for ten or twelve days before they are placed on the stage.

Several ladies and gentlemen that do not use stages, are in the habit of placing them in the front of their green-houses, in the absence of their customary plants, which at this season are set in the open air. This appears to me an excellent situation, if they are allowed air enough, not only because they are sheltered from the rain and sun, but because they are more out of the reach of the grubs, snails, and ear-wigs, provided they do not put them there sooner, nor keep them longer, than is necessary. The same remark applies with no less force to the stage. Do not, then, let the general health of your plants be endangered or injured, for the sake of preserving the blossoms unhurt.

When placed on the stage, they should have the benefit of the morning sun till about nine or ten o'clock, according to the intense heat of its rays—

D 2

the same in the evening, with as much open exposure to the air at all times as you can give them,
without injury to the bloom.

RUN FLOWERS CONSIDERED.

THERE is one subject arising out of the present, to
which I wish to call the reader's attention—a subject which, I frankly confess, I can neither compre-
hend nor explain; and the opinions that I have
ventured to offer, whether my own or borrowed, are
founded altogether on hypothesis, conjecture, and
uncertainty. What I allude to are, in the language
of a florist, the " Run-flowers."

Any one conversant with Carnations must have
remarked, in some sorts, a singular tendency to run
·from their distinct and regularly-disposed colours.
For instance, a Scarlet Bizarre, that is strongly
marked with stripes of clove colour, will frequently
change into a self-coloured flower, like the common
clove; a Purple Bizarre, in like manner, will change

to a plain purple; a Scarlet Flake to a plain scarlet,
and so on through all their varieties. A flower so
run loses all its estimation in the eyes of a florist,
and occasions him frequent regret and disappointment; for the chance of its returning to its true
colour is as one to one hundred. In fact, it may be
considered to him as lost.

> " So it falls out,
> That what we have we prize not to the worth,
> While we enjoy it; but, being lack'd and lost,
> Why then we reck the value; then we find
> The virtue, that possession would not shew us,
> While it was ours."

What is it, then, that causes this changeable disposition and suffusion of colour? Sir Humphry
Davy, perhaps, could have given a correct solution to
the question, and suggested the proper means of pre-
vention. Many attribute it to an over-richness of
the compost; that is, when too great a proportion of
dung is mixt with the loam. I am inclined to think
that there is a great degree of truth in the observation, but I am far from imagining that this is the
only cause; for I have remarked, that Carnations,

planted in the open ground in ordinary soil, will often sport, though not so frequently.

An old florist, who had grown Carnations for more than thirty years, and who had often tried them in poor soil, as well as in rich, assured me that he had found them to sport in both, but oftener in the rich; but that every season was not alike, for they would change some years more than they would in others. He concluded with this remark, that the gout would attack the poor liver as well as the rich, if there was a disposition in the body to have it; such was the case, he conceived, with the Carnation.

Some again affirm, without being able to explain the process, that it is owing to the fixed alkalis not being properly neutralized by the vegetable and vitriolic acids, that the natural colours are discharged. I confess that I am not chemist enough to understand such an operation of nature.

The summer of 1818, it will be remembered, was a very hot and dry summer, and there was a general complaint among the florists that their flowers had sported, and run from their colours, in an extraordinary degree. A neighbour of mine, who had also his share of run-flowers that summer, attributed it to his having neglected mixing slacked lime with his compost, the doing which he had not omitted, he said, for several years before.

In discoursing also with an experienced gardener the same summer on the subject, he attributed it to the powerful influence of the sun acting upon the corolla, or flower-leaves, whilst in embryo, which, he said, would start the strongest or most predominant colour, and make it suffuse and overrun the whole; for that evidently no change could take place in the plant to produce that alteration in the colour, previous to the formation of the pod, notwithstanding all the boasted prognostications about run-flowers, from redness on the joints of the stalk, and red strokes on the pod, before it opens.

After all this discussion on the subject, I believe I must leave it as I found it, uncertain and undetermined.

COMPOST FOR FLOWERS THAT ARE APT TO SPORT IN COLOUR.

As, however, it is always best and safest to be on the right side, and to adopt a system of caution in all matters where there is a degree of danger and risk to encounter, I beg to recommend a plan, which prudence suggests, and which I mean in future to adopt myself, with respect to a few sorts of the two classes of Scarlet and Crimson Bizarres, which, from their high colouring, I have found to sport more than others;—that is, to lower the compost.

I here subjoin the names of a few flowers, because they rank among the finest and best we have, viz. :—

> Humphrey's Duke of Clarence,
> James's Lord Craven,
> Hoyle's General Washington,
> Weltje's Sir Edward Pellew,
> Sharpe's Defiance,
> Plummer's Lord Manners,
> Gabell's Hero,

Cartwright's Rainbow,
Davey's Rainbow,
Phillip's Lord Harrington,
Tate's Waterloo,
Berryman's Jubilee,
Chaplain's Lord Duncan,
Cope's Suwarrow,
Stone's Venus.

℞.—3 Barrows of sound staple loam,
   1 Do. old rotten cow-dung,
   2 Do.   do.   horse-dung,
   $\frac{1}{2}$ Do. sand,
   $\frac{1}{2}$ Do. lime rubbish, or old plaster.

To be prepared, and well incorporated, as before.

It is nearly in the same proportions, and of the same component parts, as that used by the late ingenious Mr. Homes, of Clapham Common, a gentleman noted for his fine collection of tulips, and his successful cultivation of flowers in general.

THE YELLOW PICOTÉE.

THE Yellow Picotée is, at all times, a difficult flower to grow well in this country, on account of our moist atmosphere and long winters. The Dutch florists have bad success with it likewise, for the same reason. The best situation for it is the front shelf in a green-house, while in bloom, and the same place is best for it in the winter months of January and February, when it requires to be kept moderately dry; indeed it never likes to be over-saturated with water at any time. If kept in frames, during the winter, it ought to be allowed to occupy the front rows, at the back part, as being the driest and most airy. If placed in a damp situation, and over-watered, if it does not perish, it will become unsound and unhealthy, and consequently unable to carry its bloom.

It is generally scarce, for there is never any great stock of it in the country, though it is so constantly imported from the Continent, particularly by the

YELLOW PICOTE.

Pub: by Whittaker Treacher & Co Ave Maria Lane.

A Ducôte's Lithog.y 70. St Martins Lane

families of the nobility and gentry, in their excursions thither, and with whom it seems to be a very great favourite. It is to be met with in many parts of Italy, Germany, Prussia, and Flanders, in the neighbourhood of Lausanne, in Switzerland, and of Grenoble and Lyons, in the province of Dauphiny, and other parts of France.

The Empress Josephine, distinguished among other things for her great taste and fondness for flowers, had, among an endless variety of elegant and curious shrubs, plants, and flowers, an admirable collection of Yellow Picotées, at Malmaison. Her gardens were then under the superintendence of the celebrated botanist, Bonpland, who subsequently went to South America to prosecute his favourite study under the patronage of the late President Bolivar.

The late Queen Charlotte and the Princesses, a few years ago, had a very superb collection of yellow Picotées at Frogmore, which were obtained principally from Germany; they were the delight of all who saw them.

A gentleman, some time a resident in Funchal in the island of Madeira, which lies off the north-west coast of Africa, nearly opposite to Mogadore in the kingdom of Morocco, informed me, that Picotées, with yellow grounds, grew in great profusion in most of the gardens in the island, and that the varieties were beautiful; some were plain, others again were marked with red or black spots, and others curiously mottled.

This flower consists of many varieties:

Of yellow and purple, both light and dark;
    Ditto and dark red, or claret colour;
    Ditto and scarlet;
    Ditto and pink, and plain yellow of various
      shades.

Die Koeniginn Von England,	Le Dauphin de France,
Cupidon,	Prince de Condé,
Pactolus,	Count de Grasse,
Napoleon,	Prince of Orange,
El Dorado,	La Rose d'Or,
Maximilian,	Flammula,
Louis Seize,	Goldfinch,
	Maid of Magdeburg,

Maid of Orleans,   Le Cocu en colère,
Le Cocu content.   Princessinn Esterhazij,
&c. &c. &c.

I confess I am at a loss to say what compost is proper to grow it in, and yet, after all, the fault perhaps does not rest with the soil, but the climate, which, take it the year round, is too harsh and moist for this delicate exotic—yet I recommend the following :

     2 barrows of light loam,
     1   do. leaf-mould,
     1   do. old frame dung,
     $\frac{1}{2}$ do. old cow dung,
     $\frac{1}{4}$ do. river sand.

MODE OF PRESERVING THE SEED.

To any one having an opportunity of collecting any Yellow Picotée seed, which he may be desirous to bring or send to England, I recommend him to put it into a small phial or glass bottle, corked so as to exclude the air. In this state, it will keep good for a couple of years.

I have been often gratified with the sight of new yellow Picotées from the south of Germany: their colours were rich and vivid, unicolor, bicolor, and tricolor; the shape of the blossoms finely formed, and the petals large and regular. The Bizarrérie or mixture of tints in many of them was to me quite new: I have seen chocolate and yellow; pink and yellow; sulphur and crimson; buff, scarlet, and grey; yellow, purple, and white; yellow, crimson, and chocolate; yellow, slate, and grey; some with scarlet stripes upon lilac grounds; and the reverse, presenting the glossy appearance of satin. Though the colours upon the whole were very distinct, and finely traced, yet in some they were most strangely confused and oddly mixed, like a painter's delineation of fire, or rather his representation of fire and smoke, consisting of red, yellow, and ash colour, both dark and light, as in the flowers named ' Phœnix inter flammas ;' Newton and Ippersill.

Any person desirous of viewing some of these new and curious varieties, may have their desire gratified by visiting my small garden in July next, (God

granting,) for the tenure of human life is very uncertain in the most robust and healthful.

Their names run as follows :

Kaysernoon Russland,	Sophia,
Prinz Eugene,	Arthur,
—— Clemens,	Heinrich,
—— Rodolpho,	Plinius,
—— Bernhaid,	Juno,
—— Adam,	Apollo,
Fürst Lichtenstein,	Phœnix,
General Kleist,	Venus,
——— Bellegarde,	Luna,
——— Frimont,	Doernberg,
Pauline Von Russland,	Villeda,
Landgravine,	Retzau,
Belle Bergère,	Welden,
Amelia,	Gracieuse,
Agnes,	Gloriosa,
Bertha,	La Magnifique,
Maria,	Leibgardist,
Phyllis,	

and many names of individuals sounding uncouthly
in an English ear, with their official titles of Amtman,
Heptman, Rittmeister, &c. &c. prefixed.

THE OPERATION AND TIME OF PIPING.

THE propagation by piping, or cuttings, is more difficult with the Carnation than with either the Picotée or Pink, and ought to commence as soon as the shoots or grass are ready.

If you defer it till the bloom is nearly over, the chance of success is still more precarious, as the shoots get too hard and woody, and do not strike root so readily as they do when taken sooner, and in a more tender state.

The operation of piping, then, ought to commence, for the reason above stated, about the first of July. I am aware that the usual mode is to wait until the flowers are in bloom, that you may see whether they are in their right colours or not. But, surely, it is no very difficult task to guard against this, by keeping the cuttings of every plant separate. Suppose you have three plants in one pot: you can easily affix three separate tallies, or number-sticks, with 1, 2, 3, on them, and also three other corresponding tallies to the pipings. By adopting this simple method, and paying a little attention while you are about it, it will be impossible not to keep a tolerably correct account. But if you find too much trouble or difficulty in keeping such an account as I here point out, you may wait a fortnight or three weeks longer, till the flowers are in bloom—you will still be in time; but remember this, your chance of success will be less, and your plants less also. Plants raised from cuttings are, in general, preferable to those from layers, because they are sounder, and will encounter the rigours of a sharp winter better. I do not infer from this that you should pipe all the shoots, and by so great mutilation damage and disfigure the plants just coming into bloom. On the contrary, then, I recommend you to select and take the shoots only where they appear crowded or too short, or too high up the stalk to be laid easily, leaving the rest to the more certain method of laying. Carnation pipings succeed best upon a little dung-heap of blood warmth, on a bed raised two or three feet above the surface of the earth; for, should the season be wet, they are more out of the reach of the dampness of the ground, and also more exposed to the air.

Compost for piping should consist of—

$\frac{1}{3}$ Maiden earth,
$\frac{1}{3}$ Leaf mould,
$\frac{1}{3}$ Rotten horse-dung,
$\frac{1}{6}$ Sand.

To be well mixed together, and passed through a fine sieve, that the ends of the cuttings, when stuck in, may enter easily and without injury.

The piping should be cut with a sharp pen or budding knife, at the second or third joint, according to the condition of the grass; but the shorter the better. The cut must take place horizontally, close below the joint, and the sheath or part that covers the joint must be carefully removed and peeled off.

When the pipings are cut, the surface of the bed made flat and level, and gently watered through a fine rose, they may be stuck in, three-quarters of an inch deep, in rows, not too near together. Then let them be watered again, which will help to fix the earth close round them; the glasses on no account

are to be shut down close till they are dry, or they
will inevitably fog, rot, and perish. The best glasses
for piping are those made of the common window-
glass, eight inches square and six inches deep, and
the less air they contain, the sooner will the cuttings
strike root. The striking-glasses in common use,
which are blown for the purpose, too often contain
such a thick body of glass, as to concentrate the sun's
rays, and scorch the pipings. They require shading
only when the sun is out, and then with a net or old
mat, to admit the glimmering of his rays. If the
weather continues dry and hot, they will require to
be watered occasionally, with a fine rose, early in a
morning, over the glasses; which, for one fortnight
at least, need not be removed, if they are doing well.
After, you may take them off from time to time as
you see occasion, for half an hour or so in a morning,
or evening, to dry the glasses; and, if any of the
pipings appear mildewed or rotten, pull them up.
At the end of six weeks they will be sufficiently
rooted to be transplanted into small pots, or a prepared bed, over which it would be advisable to place

a frame and lights for a week or ten days, till they take root again. There they may be allowed to remain till the middle or so of September.

In taking them up, if you find any of them not rooted, but sound, and their ends hard and callow, do not let them remain on the same spot, but remove them to another bed, with a little temporary heat, and cover them with glasses as before; this will not fail to start them, and hasten their fibring.

If this method be adopted and pursued through all the minuteness of detail with which I have endeavoured to lay it down, I am confident it will succeed.

OF LAYING.

ABOUT the 21st of July your flowers will be sufficiently expanded to show which are in colour, and which not. I would then have you to prepare for laying, and to continue it as opportunity serves, till the whole be completed. They may be done with safety any time between the 21st of July and the

21st of August: but as some are more difficult and slower in striking root than others, I advise you to begin with them. I here present you with the names of a few that I have found some difficulty with; *viz.*

Davey's Sovereign,
Davey's Duchess of Devonshire,
Hoyle's Magnificent,
Lacey's Marquis of Wellesley,
Lee's Apollo,
Crump's Lord Rodney,
Lacey's Lady Wellington,
Wood's Comet,
Harley's Wonderful,
Sharpe's Defiance,
Turner's Alexander,
Turner's Hannibal.

The plants should receive a good watering the day previous to laying, because they can receive it only, for some time after, through the fine rose of the water-pot, on account of the layers.

The first step is to trim them, by cutting off with a pair of sharp scissors the leaves next the root, and about an inch in length of those at the end, moving at the same time the surface-mould in the pots, and adding to it about half an inch in thickness of your finely-sifted compost, as directed under the head of piping.

They will then be ready for the incision, which must be made with a sharp knife longitudinally, on the under side, a little below the second or third joint from the top: the knife must pass completely through the joint, and extend a quarter of an inch beyond it, forming altogether an incision of nearly an inch long, and dividing the stem of the layer in half lengthwise, as far as it goes.

The nib, or extreme end of the tongue, as it is called, must be carefully cut off, immediately below the joint; if left on, it is apt to decay, and prevent the end from becoming callow, which process must take place before the layer can form, or throw out any fibres. The tongue must be fixed downwards in the mould, and secured in that position, with a fern or wooden peg made for the purpose, and the joint where the cut took place covered about three-quarters of an inch deep with the fine mould. Should the part that is pegged down be washed bare at any time by watering, it must be again covered with a little more mould.

If the weather prove in any degree favourable, they will be fit to take off in seven or eight weeks; when they may be planted, two or three in an upright 48 pot, or two in a 60, according to their size. Let them be set upon tiles, slates, or boards, to prevent the worms getting into the pots, in which situation they may be suffered to remain till the middle or end of October, according to the state of the weather, which is about the usual period of putting them in their winter quarters, where they are to remain till spring. As soon as the layers are rooted and fit to take off, they should be potted, to enable the fibres to get established before the cold weather sets in; the removal, if possible, should not be deferred later than Michaelmas.

Observe not to plant the layers too deep or low down in the pots, for whatever part of the side foliage is buried or covered will decay and rot, to the no small injury of the whole.

WINTER SITUATION.

It may, perhaps, be considered not improper to give a few cautionary hints respecting their treatment during their inactive state in the winter.

It is usual to put about four inches deep of coal-ashes at the bottom of the frames, for the pots to stand upon; this keeps out the worms, and at the same time protects the fibres during very severe weather: they should be placed also pretty near the glass. Let them have all the benefit of the air you can, by drawing the lights quite off in dry weather, and by giving air behind in wet. In frosty weather, which is not very severe, they should be exposed to the air, especially a few hours in the middle of the day.

It is also an excellent plan to rest the frames upon bricks, to let in a free circulation of air below, among the pots; the frames in some seasons may remain raised in this manner even till Christmas: for it is quite time enough to remove the bricks, and let the frames down close to the ground, when the frost appears to set in.

The safest method, perhaps, is to keep them moderately dry in the months of December and January; and when they require water, give it them through the narrow pipe of a small water-pot, instead of the rose. If watered with the rose, unless there be a brisk air and a little sun to dry the plants, the drops will hang upon them for several days together, and spot and mildew the leaves; indeed it is never right to shut them down close when wet. About once in six weeks, as you see occasion, take a small pointed stick, and lightly stir the mould on the surface, to prevent any green and sour incrustation taking place. Many cover the tops of the pots with a little fine sand. The decayed leaves should also be taken off from time to time. Should the weather be temperate and mild, with any gentle rains from the south or south-west, they should be permitted to receive the benefit of them for half an hour or so, five or six times during the winter; this will greatly refresh them, taking care to have their

E

leaves dried again as soon as you can. If kept too
dry any length of time together, I have observed
that the stem loses its pith, and becomes like a dry
hollow reed: steer between the two extremes, and
you will do right.

ON SEED AND SEEDLINGS.

I HAVE already transgressed the limits which I had
prescribed to myself in setting out; I will therefore
close the subject with a few cursory remarks on
Seed and Seedlings.

The Carnation is not a prolific seed-bearer: it
often happens, that out of two hundred blooming
plants, you will not be able to get even two pods of
perfect seed. The reason may be accounted for in
this way: first, because it is a flower that blows late
in the summer, and has not time always to ripen its
seed, especially in a wet one; secondly, because the
Carnations that are usually cultivated are so very
double, as to preclude in a great measure the ex-

pectancy of much seed; it is the semi-double flowers
that yield the most. In the year 1818, more seed,
I believe, was saved that summer than in any seven
preceding put together; it was excessively hot, and
the heat continued till the autumn. There is hardly
a Carnation-grower in the country that has not
raised seedling-plants from seed saved that summer;
but as it is two years before they bloom, he will have
to wait till the ensuing summer before he can have
an opportunity of ascertaining their worth.

The Carnation is a variable flower, and the inconstancy of its seed is equal only to the variety produced from it. It is said, but I know not with what
truth, that seed out of the same pod will produce
flowers of all the different varieties—flakes, bizarres,
&c., both single, semi-double, and double. Several
superior flowers have been produced from seed saved
from Gregory's King Alfred, Lacey's Marquis of
Wellesley, Crump's Lord Rodney, Butts's Lord
Rodney, Stoniard's Britannia, Bearliss's Sir G.
Osborn, Onion's Trafalgar, &c.

If you perceive the pericarpium or seed vessel to

swell and grow hard, so as to give hopes of seed, which it will not do till the flower is fading, and the leaves of it withering, then pluck the petals one by one out of the corolla or cup, taking great care not to injure the styles, or two horns, which if you do, all chance of seed is lost. By letting the flower-leaves remain in the cup, they are apt to hold the dew and wet, which frequently occasions the whole to rot. As the seed vessel fills up, you may with a pair of scissors cut off the ends of the cup all round, and make a slight incision down it, to keep the wet from resting in it. It will ripen towards the end of September; but do not gather it till it is fully ripe, when it will be of a dark brown or black colour. It is the safest way to let it remain in the seed-pod, in some dry place, till after Christmas, when it may be cleaned, and put into a paper bag, or small bottle.

It may be sown in wide pans, or 24-sized pots, about the second week in April, which is quite early enough, and covered a quarter of an inch thick with fine mould, the surface to be made smooth and level, both before and after sowing. Hand-glasses may be placed over them till it comes up, which will also prevent the heavy rains from washing it out of the ground. If the plants are in too forward a state, and their growth too much accelerated by watering during the summer, they are apt to spindle, that is, every shoot nearly will run up to flower, scarcely leaving one to propagate from.

I do not wish to discourage the young florist in his attempts to raise Seedling Carnations; but he will find the production of fine flowers to be a work of time, patience, and uncertainty. If I set a ratio as one to one hundred, I fear the calculation will be too extravagant, and that I shall not be borne out in it by the fact; but let him look upon the whole as a lottery, and if fortune favours him, he may perhaps win two capital prizes, or more. The production of one superior flower—it is folly to keep an inferior one in the present highly improved breed of Carnations—will no doubt afford him much pleasure and gratification; but if he should be fortunate enough to raise six during the whole course of his life, he must consider his labours to have been crowned with success; and as vanity and self-conceit, which spring from ignorance, are apt to blind and mislead the judgment in all matters that concern ourselves, I caution the florist who has raised any Seedling Carnations, not to be too hasty in pronouncing upon their excellence, but submit them to the inspection and criticism of another as well as himself, lest while he fancies he is breeding up a swan, it should prove at last to be nothing but a goose. A bad florist is nearly in the same situation as a bad poet,—he becomes the butt of ridicule, and his productions the subject of derision and contempt.

THE PICOTEE, AND THE REASON OF ITS PARTIAL EXCLUSION FROM THE STAGE.

ONE thing respecting Seedlings had nearly escaped my recollection, which is this:—Most florists, whose views are principally directed to the raising of fine flowers from seed, exclude the Picotée, with its spotted leaves and indented edges, from the society of the Carnation altogether, lest the farina or pollen of the Picotée should become impregnated with that of the Carnation, and so spoil its breed. This opinion seems generally to prevail, and I am not prepared with any argument that can counteract it.

For my part, however, no such consideration shall ever induce me to exclude from the garden, or to forego the pleasure of beholding, the varied, the fanciful, and beautiful blossom of the Picotée, which presents itself in all the delicate and softer tints of the Carnation, not indeed disposed with that preciseness and regularity, but pencilled and marked by the inimitable hand of Nature in her more sportive mood: at one time, on a snow-white ground, a vast profusion of small, irregular spots appear — red, black, or purple; at another, a few straight lines or dashes of the pencil only are seen on some of the larger petals; then a fanciful mixture of both together, most beautifully blended; at another time, the edges or extremity only of the flower-leaves shall be tinged and laced all round, or the whole covered

with a netted and motley mixture of shining colours.

I have often remarked the preference given to
Picotées by most ladies : after being tired with
gazing at the gaudy and more dazzling beauties of
the Carnation, they have turned, with apparently
greater satisfaction, to examine and admire the soft
and delicate graces of their favourite Picotée.

ON THE PLAGIARISM, &c. OF FLORISTS.

THERE is another topic connected with the present
subject which in a manner forces itself upon me,
yet it is with some degree of reluctance that I enter
upon it.

The florists, no doubt, are a race of men subject
to the same passions as other men are; and these
passions, even in the florist, if they are suffered, like
weeds, to run riot, and are not properly pruned and
restrained, will sometimes prompt him to commit
actions, which are not strictly compatible with the
innocent and pleasing avocation which he pursues.

Gentle reader, be not alarmed; I am not going to charge him with the dreadful crimes of murder or manslaughter, notwithstanding the deep scarlet and crimson hues with which those flowers are stained that he often holds in his hands. No; I charge him only, as a lawyer might express it, if he belonged to that learned body, with certain malpractices in his profession, which I think it my duty to mention, that they may be exposed, and the authors of them, when detected, held up to ridicule and contempt.

What I mean by all this preamble is neither more nor less than this—that a florist will sometimes, either with a view to raise his reputation, or from the more sordid motive of gain, procure from some distant part of the country the favourite and admired flower of another, under its true name; he will then christen it afresh, and palm it upon the public as a seedling Carnation of his own.

He will not unfrequently also substitute, in the way of trade, one flower for another, seldom a better for a worse, to the great disappointment and vexation of the person so receiving it. This is the reason why we so often find the same flower under different names, of which I could point out instances not a few. Thus we have two Rainbows, as two may sometimes be seen in the heavens at the same time; but then the one is only the faint shadow and reflection of the other. So we have two James's Lord Craven, two Castle's Mrs. Barrington, two Sharpe's Defiance, two or three Weltje's Pellew, two or three Young's Mount Ætna, &c. &c.

But, what is worse than all, it is also said that he will sometimes not hesitate to sell and deliver a run flower, instead of one in colour, knowing it to be so. Such unfair practices as these must, however, in the end, defeat themselves; and let us hope that they are confined but to a few, and do not apply to the body of florists in general.

A STAGE OF CARNATIONS.

A STAGE of Carnations is a splendid and beautiful sight, of which no one can form any just idea, unless he has had the opportunity of beholding two or three hundred blossoms at one time.

Sarah, Duchess of Marlborough, was extremely partial to Carnations, and had every year about two hundred pots of them : she was frequently heard to say, that nothing gave her so much pleasure as the sight of her Carnations in full bloom, and which she preferred to all the green-house plants in her possession.

Sir John Hill, also, in some of his works, speaks in praise of the Carnation, whose fragrance, he says, led him to enjoy it frequently. There is not the least doubt but that it has been the distinguished favourite of thousands, in all ages and in all countries, wherever it could be met with, from the earliest times down to the present; and a singular predilection in its favour at the present day seems to be

manifested among all ranks throughout the kingdom, by whom it is equally cherished and cultivated.

Hear what that political Proteus, yet clever writer,
Mr. Cobbett, says of a Carnation, to which he attri-
butes beauty and fragrance in the highest degree.
' Some persons may think that flowers are things of
' no use—that they are nonsensical things; the same
' may be, and perhaps with more reason, said of ·
' pictures. An Italian, while he gives his fortune
' for a picture, will laugh to scorn a Hollander, who
' leaves a tulip-root as a fortune to his son. For my
' part, as a thing to keep, and not to sell,—as a thing,
' the possession of which is to give me pleasure,—I
' hesitate not a moment to prefer the plant of a fine
' Carnation to a gold watch set with diamonds.'
And he continues, ' Those who have once seen a
. ' bed of beautiful Tulips, Carnations, or Auriculas,
' enjoy during life the delightful sight in recollection.'

The effect produced by a number of Carnations
together is undoubtedly striking; and it is beauty in
masses only that can produce such an effect.

The Clove Gilliflower, or the true Old Clove, as

it is called, and of which we hear so much mention made, if we may credit the testimony of very old gardeners, is now lost to the country. One flower, they will tell you, would scent the whole garden, the perfume was so strong and powerful. It may be so; I have not the means of contradicting it.

THE DUTCH MODE OF GARDENING.

WE are apt to ridicule the Dutchman, as well as the imitators of him here at home, who divide their gardens into small beds, or compartments, planting each with separate and distinct flowers. We ridicule the plan, because it exhibits too great a sameness and formality; like unto the nosegay that is composed of one sort of flowers only, however sweet and beautiful they may be, they lose the power to please, because they want variety. It must undoubtedly be acknowledged, that a parterre, no matter in what form—whether circular or square, elliptical or oblong

—where all the shrubs, plants, and flowers in it, like
the flowers of a tastefully-arranged bouquet, are va-
riously disposed in neat and regular order, according
to their height and colour, is a delightful spectacle,
and worthy of general imitation. Yet still in some
particular cases I am disposed to copy the Dutchman, and I would have my bed of Hyacinths distinct, my Tulips distinct, my Anemonies, my Ranunculuses, my Pinks, my Carnations distinct, and
even my beds of Double Blue Violets and Dwarf
Larkspurs distinct, to say nothing of hedge-rows of
different sorts of Roses: independent of the less
trouble you have in cultivating them when kept separate, you have, as I said before, beauty in masses,
and you have likewise their fragrance and perfume
so concentrated, that they are not lost in air, but
powerfully inhaled when you approach them.

In support of the above argument, I beg to quote
an authority of no small consideration.

Mrs. Siddons, the celebrated tragic actress, was a
great admirer of this mode of planting, and fond of
contemplating this ' beauty in masses.' She adopted

this style of gardening at her late residence on the Harrow-road. One favourite flower with her was the Viola Amœna, the Pansy*, or Common Purple Heart's-ease, and this she set with unsparing profusion all around her garden. Her great and constant call for this flower every spring, to keep the purple bordering complete and perfect, induced the gardeners in the neighbourhood to give the name of Miss Heart's-ease to her managing handmaid, who used to chaffer for it in the true spirit of hard and thrifty dealing. Her garden was remarkable in another respect, and might with great propriety be styled a garden of evergreens, which, together with a few deciduous shrubs, were of the most sombre, sable, and tragical cast—such as Box-trees, Fir, Privet, Phillyrea, Arbor Vitæ, Holly, Cypress, the Red Cedar, Laurel, Irish Ivy, Bay-tree, Arbutus Daphne, or Spurge Laurel, Cneorum Tricoccum, or the 'Widow-Wail,' the branches and flowers of

---

* Pansy, Panacea, derived from the Greek, signifying Heal-all.

which, according to Pliny, were carried by the Roman matrons in their funeral processions :—

'Purpureos spargam flores.'—VIRGIL.

The only part of the year in which it could be viewed with any degree of satisfaction was the winter, as giving rise to a pleasing association of ideas, in beholding these retain their green verdure and clothing at a time when the rest of the surrounding trees were stripped naked and bare.

In addition to what I have already stated, I cannot help making mention of a large bed of Hollyhocks (the Alcea Rosea, a native of China), which I noticed some few years ago in the gardens of Messrs. Lee and Kennedy, of Hammersmith. I think I counted in the bed fourteen distinct varieties of this beautiful species, of tall and short growth; the flowers were all double, and the effect produced by them was grand beyond description.

The immense number of rose-shaped blossoms, and the strong contrast of their shades and colours —white, yellow, red, crimson, brown, black, &c., arrested my attention; I thought this group of flowers at the time one of the finest and most magnificent sights I had ever witnessed.

CARNATION BED.

FLORISTS in general have a greater stock of Carnations than they find convenient to blow in pots, and these they plant out in the ground towards the latter end of March. There is no doubt but that they might do equally as well, if they were planted in the open ground about the beginning of October, and would stand through the winter unhurt, provided a slight protection could be afforded them by mats, or a piece of sail-cloth thrown over them, resting on hoops, during continued rains, heavy falls of snow, or other severe weather; but they who have the means of wintering them in frames seldom run that risk, and prefer planting them out in the spring.

The pains which they bestow in preparing and

making the bed for them, depend in a great measure
on the value they set on the plants; if they are some
of their choice sorts, and they are anxious to have
fine blooms, they will form a fresh bed altogether.
In this case, they first remove a foot in depth of the
old earth, and then dig over what remains to the
depth of a foot more, provided there be that depth
before they come to the subsoil; they will then cover
the surface with a stratum of rotten horse-dung, three
inches deep, not too much exhausted—that which
comes directly from the cucumber-bed is to be preferred; they will then replace the mould which they
removed in the first instance, with the same sort of
compost as is intended for the Carnations in pots,
raising the bed about four inches above the surface
of the ground, and rounding the top a little in a
convex form, just enough to give the water a gentle
descent each way. If the bed is four feet wide, it
will contain four rows, if the plants are set singly,
but only three if set in pairs, as turned out of the
pots, allowing sufficient room for laying.

I need scarcely repeat here that they will require

a plentiful supply of water, as they come into flower, to swell the pod, and to increase the blossom.

The following Catalogue of Carnations and Picotées comprehends the greatest part of the choicest flowers in England.

CARNATIONS.

SCARLET BIZARRES.

Astin's Lord Exmouth

Bray's Defiance

· Broadbent's Victorious

Brown's Lord Hood

———— Lord Nelson

Barefield's Lord Nelson

Bigg's Don Cossack

———— Defiance

Bate's Regent

———— Nelson

Brady's Bravo

Barker's Sovereign

Cartwright's Abercrombie

· Clarke's Regent

Costin's Monarch

Craddock's Sir Sidney Smith

Crump's Lord Rodney

Colcutt's Emperor

Cook's Wellington

Davey's Cæsar Augustus

———— Sovereign

———— Honourable Thos. Brand

Gabell's Hero

Hall's Champion

Hoyle's General Washington

Harley's Waterloo

———— Generalissimo

———— Earl of Oxford

Humphrey's Duke of Clarence

Handy's Regent

Hine's Duke of Wellington

—— Lord Exmouth

Hogg's Lord Sydney

——— Duke of Montrose

——— Epaminondas

Houghton's Duke of Newcastle

James's Lord Craven

Lee's British Beauty

—— Lord Byron

—— Emperor Alexander

Leigh's Wellington

Lisset's Seedling

Mason's Sovereign

——— Lord Compton

Martin's Matchless

——— Macbeth

Notcutt's Lord Mansfield

—— Lord St. Vincent

Onion's Hero of Trafalgar

Plummer's Lord Manners

Pope's Lord Hood

Pearson's Chilwell Hero

——— Blucher

——— Lord Bagot

Reynold's King

Smalley's Foxhunter

Sharpe's Defiance

Smedmore's Regent

Snook's Charles Fox

——— Paragon

——— Defiance

——— John Bull

Strong's Victorious

Smith's Emperor

Stourbridge Regulator

Tallis's Prince William Henry

Turner's Alexander

——— Blucher

——— Sir Francis Burdett

Taylor's Lord Nelson

Waterhouse's Rising Sun

Weltje's Buonaparte

——— Sir Edward Pellew

——— No. 23

——— Sir Sidney Smith

Walker's Defiance

——— Hero

——— Monarch

——— Pageant

Webb's Duke of Wellington

Warman's Captain Wise

Wood's Lord Nelson
Waters' Prince of Wales
Young's Mount Ætna

Young's British Hero.
Yeomanson's Eclipse
——— ——— Triumphant

CRIMSON BIZARRES.

Astin's Marquis of Anglesea
Bate's Magnificent
Bugbird's Sir F. Burdett
Bond's Agenora
Brown's Defiance
——— Lord Nelson
Barker's Sir Robert Wilson
Brook's Adonis
Bailey's Wellington
Berriman's Jubilee
Cartwright's Rainbow
——— ——— Supreme
Crook's Marquis
Chaplin's Admiral Duncan
Cope's Suwarrow
Christian's Superb
Davey's King David
——— Rainbow
Fletcher's Staffordshire
Hero
Gregory's King Alfred
——— Patriot

Gabell's Esquire Garle
Hopkin's King Solomon
Horrock's Collingwood
——— Prince Leopold
Hoyle's Magnificent
Howarth's Grenadier
Harley's Diana
——— Lord Lough-
borough
——— Cockade
Hogg's Hamlet
——— Adventurer
——— John Goldham,
Esq.
——— King George IV.
Lacey's Marquis of Wel-
lesley
Lacy's Waterloo
Lee's Duke of Bridgewater
——— Apollo
——— Duke of Kent
——— King George

Martin's King Arthur
———— Earl Grey
———— Duke of Grafton
———— Marquis of Bath
———— Glory, *four distinct
  colours*
———— British Farmer
———— Lord Erskine
———— Dundee Beauty
Miller's Champion
———— Joe Miller
———— St. George
Phillip's Lord Harrington
Pearson's Lord Middleton
———— Superb
———— No. 3
Quarterman's Oxford Hero

Steed's Yorkshire Hero
Snook's Emperor
Smedmore's Lord Nelson
Stretch's King
Toule's Sir John Leicester
Terry's King
Troup's Beauty
Tate's Waterloo
——— Yorkshire Lad
Walker's Marquis
———— Baron
Wallace's Sir Wm. Wallace
Yeomanson's Coburg
———— Magnificent
———— General Picton
———— Lord Hill

PURPLE BIZARRES.

Hine's British Farmer | Hogg's Sir Joseph Banks

PINK AND PURPLE BIZARRES.

Astin's Victory
Bowstead's Queen
———— Hero
Bate's Duchess of York

Bearless's Sir Geo. Osborne
Church's Seedling
Davey's Duchess of Devonshire

Davey's Lady Grey
Davis's Regent
French's Duke of Kent
Fryer's King
Gill's Bristol Hero
Harcourt's Prince of Wales
Hogg's Dulce Decus
Kenny's Patriot
Mason's Seedling
Pephall's Oldenburgh
Pearson's Eminent

Troup's Hero
———— Duke of Gloucester
———— Duke of Wellington
Tucker's Duchess of Devonshire
Weltje's Maid of Honour
Walker's Buckingham
———— Pilgrim
Wallace's Lady Duncan

SCARLET FLAKES.

Astin's Seedling
Brook's Colonel Tarleton
Belcher's Lady Spenser
Barker's Mrs. Clarke
Barr's Waterloo
Barnes's Lord Nelson
Cartwright's Commander
———— Pirate
Davis's Sir William Curtis
Eagleton's Marquis of Tavistock
Fulbrook's Lord Nelson
Harley's Enchanter
———— Regent

Harley's Wonderful
Hogg's Sirius
———— Mount Hecla
Hill's Marquis of Anglesea
Incomparable Dutch Flake
James's Prince of Wales
Lee's Queen
Lyford's Regent
Lacey's Queen
———— Lady Wellington
Mason's Duke of Wellington
———— Duke of Devonshire

Martin's Morning Star
———— Earl of Leven
Page's Queen Caroline
Pearson's Juno
———— —— Rising Sun
Snook's No. 12
———— Lord John Russell
Strong's Lady Romilly
Stoinard's Britannia
Thornicroft's Blucher
———————— Britannia
———— —— Superb
———— —— Brilliant
———————— Victory
———————— Venus

Tagg's Glory of Oxford
Walker's Emerald
———— Ruby
Wood's Comet
Wilson's Lord Nelson
Winter's Berkshire Flamingo
Waterhouse's Queen Caroline
——————— Duke of Norfolk
——————— Earl Fitzwilliam
Yeomanson's Blucher
———————— Commander

PURPLE FLAKES.

Adwin's Princess Royal
Barker's Top Sawyer
Butt's Lord Rodney
Brown's British Beauty
Bates' Wellington
Boyle's Lord Ashbrook
Cartwright's Seedling
Castle's Mrs. Barrington
Cornfield's Sir George Robinson

Crook's Royal Purple
Cope's Miss Platoff
Dickson's Mary Queen of Scots
———— Fame
Fulbrook's Grenadier
Gardiner's Trimmer
Houghton's Miss Saville
Hoyle and Boad's Queen
Hardman's Lord Exmouth

Honey's Princess Charlotte
Hogg's Mrs. Siddons
————— Pilot
Harley's Smuggler
James's Queen
Lester's Purple Flake
Page's Seedling
Porter's Queen
Palmer's Defiance
————— Duchess of Dorset
Patson's Marlborough
Phillip's Defiance
————— Britannia
Redfern's Derby Hero
Stable's Queen

Strong's Eliza
Turner's Hannibal
Taylor's Waterloo
Williams's Duchess of York
Walker's British Beauty
————— Columbine
Wright's Duchess of Man-
  chester
Wood's Ambassador
————— Aid-de-camp
————— Princess Charlotte
————— Commander
Waterhouse'sIncomparable
Wilde's Mary Ann

ROSE AND PINK FLAKES.

Astin's Lady Paget
Barr's Rose Flake
Brook's Rosy Bacchus
Crooke's Duchess of Wel-
  lington
————— Lady Mildmay
————— Roi des Roses
Cartwright's Rosa
————— Juliet
Davey's Lady Shannon

Davey's Tower of Babel
Davis's Princess Charlotte
————— Princess of Wales
————— Duchess of York
Fletcher's Duchess of De-
  vonshire
Gabell's Islington Beauty
Harley's Mrs. Clarke
Hine's Queen
Hogg's Paddington Beauty

Hogg's Queen
—— Miss Cockerill
—— Lady Burgoyne
—— Galatea
Hoyle's Beauty
Honey's General Elliot
Lacey's Princess of Wales
—— Marchioness of
    Wellesley
Metcalf's Miss Saunders
Martin's Lady Exmouth
Meesom's Invincible
Mason's Queen Caroline
—— Duchess of Glou-
    cester
Martin's Isabella Martin
—— Lady Grey
Newland's Beauty
Plummer's Lord Keith

Pearson's Lady Loudon
Piannon's Lord Norris
Rivers' Incomparable
Snook's Queen Caroline
Smedmore's Duchess of
    Devonshire
—— Lady Derby
Tate's Jubilee
Taylor's Staffordshire Lass
Thornicroft's Lady North-
    ampton
Walker's Fairy Queen
—— Rosamond
Warman's Miss Ormond
Wild's Cottage Girl
Wood's Aurora
Yeomanson's Duchess of
    Rutland
—— Helen

FRENCH CARNATIONS.

Duc d'Angoulême
Flora

Violet de Metz
Henri de Prusse

&c. &c.

Additional Catalogue of some few new varieties of Carnations, which may justly be classed among the first-rate flowers.

SCARLET BIZARRES.

Finmore's Rising Sun
Hogg's Sheriff Whittaker
Hufton's 'Squire Mundy
Landon's Falstaff
Lee's King Alfred
Mason's Achilles
———— Lord Harrington
———— Sir George Crewe
Plant's Sir John Boughey

Pearson's Competitor
Pyke's Champion
——— Gladiator
Strong's King
———— Duke of York
Thompson's Ralph Cartwright, Esq.
Roby's Salamander

CRIMSON BIZARRES.

Booth's Justice Trafford
Franklin's Queen
Hattersley's Freedom
Hufton's Miss Mundy
Ive's Leopold
Medwin's Lord Eldon
Mason's Favourite

Mason's Cam Hobhouse
Pittman's Rising Sun
Strong's Prince of Denmark
——— Linnæus
Thompson's Sir J. Miller
Yeomanson's G. Rex IV.

PURPLE BIZARRES.

Hines's Duchess of Kent
——— Lady Macclesfield

Strong's Dr. Franklin
Pyke's Eminent

SCARLET FLAKES.

Cartwright's Duke of Sussex	Strong's Emperor
Hufton's Miss Barwell	Thomson's Warrior
Mason's Eclipse	Wharton's Phœnix

PURPLE FLAKES.

Archer's Union	Strong's Esther
Mason's Lady Harrington	The Worcester Violet
Pyke's Cato	Timmis's Lord Byron
Harley's Commodore	

ROSE FLAKES.

Hale's Miss Cox	Mason's Lady Scarsdale
Houghton's Duchess of Newcastle	Thomson's Maria

It gives me pleasure to add my small tribute of praise here in behalf of Finmore's Rising Sun, Mason's Achilles, Strong's Prince of Denmark, and his Esther, Pittman's Rising Sun, Mason's Eclipse, and Wharton's Phœnix. Though this may appear somewhat invidious, where the whole are so fine, yet these last are, in my opinion, most excellent, and not to be surpassed.

BRANCH AND BLOSSOM.

' Pray, Master Blossom, are you not rather lavish of your praise? What can you know yet of these new flowers?—have you proved them sufficiently, that you speak in such good round set terms of their excellence? If you wish the world to believe that you possess some little taste and judgment, I advise you to express your sentiments with more caution and reserve, lest they should be called in question hereafter.'

' Why, Branch, have they not proved themselves already? But I know your fond partiality to your old favourites, and your great reluctance to admit of any excellence in any of the new ones. There's your favourite Pellew, if you get him good once in seven years it is as much as you do; as for old Washington, with all his reputation, if the summer proves wet, does he not then come pouncy as brickdust? See the trouble there is with Clarence, fine as he is, to keep him in health: I may say the same with

respect to Sharpe's Defiance; and as for Sovereign,
he was never half a good one.'

' Bless me, Master Blossom! do I hear such language from you ?   There's treason and treachery in
the very sound of it: I cannot listen with patience;'
for have not I heard you praise those old flowers as
much as I have ever done ? '

' And so you may again; but surely I may have
the liberty to express what I think of these new seedlings, which deservedly claim admiration.   What
proof can you want?

' Has not this modern Achilles bravely fought his
way into notice, and beat his opponents with ease ?
Has not Finmore's Rising Sun exalted himself by
his splendour and magnitude, and outshone all his
competitors ? and has not Pittman's Rising Sun also
been the envy and admiration of all that came within
the view of his broad illumined disk for three years
past?   Has not Strong's Prince of Denmark con-
ducted himself like a true and valiant prince, and
carried off, more than once, the palm of victory ?
and has not his lovely Esther, arrayed in pure white

and shining purple, with her goodly figure and attractive graces, won universal admiration? As for Mason's Eclipse, mind if he does not put the extinguisher over a good many; and lovely Phœnix, I have no doubt, will prove herself a complete " *rara avis*," and find admirers in plenty; to say nothing of Strong's Linnæus, Pyke's Champion, Thompson's 'Squire Cartwright, Hufton's Miss Mundy, Schole's Delight, &c., which are all first-rate flowers.'

' Well, well, neighbour Blossom, remember the old saying, " the least said the soonest mended :" it will be well if you are not obliged to retract some part of your opinion in this instance, as you have done in others; for I have heard you say, that you could not credit the evidence even of your own senses in respect to flowers, they present such different appearances at different seasons, and that you have been sadly deceived thereby.'

' Branch, I admit it, and moreover confess, notwithstanding all you can urge, that I would not part with Pittman's Rising Sun, though I could get in its stead the far-famed " Cravo do Duque" of Portugal, the great favourite of the Cardinal Patriarch—a flower worthy, as he says, of being presented to the Queen of Heaven. How many have sought after it in vain, his Eminence having interdicted its going among heretics! and, what is also equally strange, his gardener having had the virtue to reject the pressing offer of a handful of crusadoes and milreas for it.'

' 'Tis very well that something new turns up every season, to keep the votaries of Flora and her fancy alive. Last year, Cartwright's Rainbow, Houghton's Duchess of Newcastle, Queen Caroline, the Smuggler, and the Foxhunter took the lead; this year you have other favourites. May I ask, Mr. Blossom, what price you set on Pittman's flower, which, in your opinion, is so complete an ultra, or, as I would express it, quite an out-and-outer—a *chef-d'œuvre* of Nature?'

' That of a sovereign, at least: know, Branch, that in my impatience to obtain it, I last year offered two for it.'

' Aye, aye, money and wit seldom go together,

though I have heard it said that it is a general rule in Paddington to measure a man's intellects by the depth and weight of his purse.'

' Pooh, pooh! let us close this parley; for our hearers are, I dare say, pretty well tired.'

' With all my heart; only tell me, Master Blossom, is it true that a London tradesman has no conscience? Excuse me, I don't mean a London florist.'

' Why, Branch, as for that, a tradesman's conscience, and the consciences of his customers, are too often nearly upon a par: the one thinks he never can charge enough, and the other thinks it never time to pay.'

PICOTÉES.

.•. MY COLLECTION OF PICOTÉES IS UNRIVALLED FOR BEAUTY AND VARIETY.

Archbishop of York	Baron's Miss Neville
——— of Canterbury	Brook's Seedling
Brown's Wonderful	Bambury's Duchess of
Bartlett's Beauty	Beaufort
Barclay's Lady Dundas	Bailey's Beauty

Blaize's Blazing Star
Cartwright's Circassian
———— Pomona
Cornfield's Mr. Ponsonby
———— Lady Gardner
———— Lady Miller
———— Marchioness of
    Bath
———— Lady Christie
———— Lord Milton
———— Defiance
———— Mungo Park
———— Queen Caroline
———— Lady North-
    ampton
———— Lord Exmouth
———— Invincible
———— Prince Leopold
———— Brunette
———— Blucher
———— Highlander
———— Sir Wm. Harper
———— Duchess of Bed-
    ford
———— Duke of Bedford
Davey's Eclipse
———— True Briton
———— Lady Craven
Douglas's Duchess of Kent

Douglas's Lady Pierpont
———— Princess Char-
    lotte
———— Lady Nugent
———— Duchess of
    Gloucester
Duborg's Elegant
Furze's Superb
Hall's Morning Star
———— Lady Crewe
Hogg's Arab
———— Duke of Sussex
———— Stella
———— Lady Smith
———— Great Favourite
———— Emma
———— Louisa
———— Beauty
———— Fragrant
———— Pomona
———— Emblem of Purity
———— Sophia of Glou-
    cester
———— Princess Augusta
———— Garrick
———— Corinthian
———— Cottage Maid
———— Belvedere
Hufton's Magnum Bonum

Kenny's Superb
—— Queen
—— Incomparable
Lacey's Queen
Lawrence's Hampton Beauty
Lee's Robin Hood
—— Splendid
—— Little John
—— Colonel Stanton
—— Zebra
Montford's Hero
Mason's Wellington
—— Black Prince
—— Exmouth
—— Regent
—— Princess Charlotte
—— Princess of Wales
—— Favourite
—— Beauty
Martin's Hero
—— Ruby
—— Waterloo
—— Coburg
—— Magnificent
—— Miss Bouverie
—— Queen

Martin's Triumphant
—— Veteran
Miller's Perfect Beauty
—— True Blue
—— True Briton
Pemberton's Georgina
Pearson's Maria
—— Chillwell Beauty
—— Fair Play
Pyke's Beauty
Rouce's Lady Warren
Sandael's Litchfield Hero
Syrett's Lady Effingham
—— Lady Howard
—— Princess of Wales
—— Mars
Steed's Artaxerxes
Stone's Sparkler
—— Brilliant
—— General Picton
Spratt's Lord Effingham
Smalley's Cynthia
Woodford's Queen
Wollard's Waterloo
Yeomanson's Beauty
—— Invincible

OF THE PINK.

———

LET your Pink bed be constructed upon the same principle as that for Carnations; for to give instructions for the growth of one is to give instructions for the growth of the others—their nature and habits are alike; they require the same open situation, and the same richness of soil, and these you must let them have, if you mean to grow them in any perfection.

The Pinks must also be shaded when in bloom, if you wish their beauty to continue any length of time untarnished : either rain or sun will alike sully and fade their colour. The pods should be tied round after the manner of Carnations, with a little bass-mat, to prevent their bursting, and their number reduced, to increase the size of those you leave on.

As the Pink is earlier than the Carnation, of course the time of propagating it will be earlier also, which is generally performed by pipings or cuttings any time about the 21st of June.

When the pipings have taken root, they must be pricked out into a kind of nursery-bed, to get strength and grow, till about the middle of September, which is the customary time of planting them out in a bed, where they are to remain to flower.

It has been very frequently remarked that Pinks moved and transplanted in the spring never do well, nor show half the beauty which those do that were planted in September; the laced Pinks, in particular, appear almost plain, and without their distinguishing character. They should likewise never be suffered to remain longer than two years in the same spot and ground, without either change of soil or situation. To say more concerning Pinks I conceive wholly unnecessary; for if you have attended with any care to the directions given for the management of the Carnations, you will be at no loss how to treat them.

OF SEED.

To save seed from Pinks, you must extract the flower-leaves when they begin to wither, and pursue the same plan as is recommended with respect to Carnation seed.

Davey's Venus and Incomparable, Dakin's Burdett, Turner's Regent, and Brown's Beauty, are fine flowers to save seed from.

To the above short account I beg leave to add a letter on the culture of Pinks, which, in the year 1821, I had the honour of addressing to Joseph Sabine, Esq., Secretary to the London Horticultural Society : it was approved by the Council, and ordered to be printed in their Transactions of that year.

‘ Sir :—I feel obliged to you for the favourable
‘ opinion you were pleased to express of the few spe-
‘ cimens of Pink Blooms (for which I received the
‘ Banksian medal), which I had the honour to
‘ exhibit at a late meeting of the Horticultural So-
‘ ciety. The health of the plants, and the beauty of

' the blossoms, I attribute mainly to the mode of culti-
' vation which I pursued with respect to them; a brief
' account of which I now subjoin, hoping, though
' the subject-matter be trifling and unimportant in
' itself, that it will afford some gratification to those
' members of the Society who are fond of flowers;
' and who feel pleasure in the admiration, at least,
' if not in the cultivation of them.

' I formed my Pink beds and planted them about
' the middle of October; they were raised six inches
' above the alleys, to enable the heavy rains to pass
' off during the winter. The soil consisted of a
' sandy loam, or, more correctly speaking, of a com-
' mixture of yellowish loam, common black garden-
' mould, road grit taken from the entrance to the
' Paddington pond, which might not improperly be
' called sand, having been washed by the water;
' and a good portion of rotten horse-dung, well in-
' corporated, with a good bottom of dung from the
' cucumber pits: added to which, I top-dressed the
' beds in the beginning of May, after weeding and
' lightly hoeing the surface, with nearly an inch

' thick of rotten dung passed through a coarse sieve,
' in which was a small quantity of one-year old
' sheep-dung, the sweepings of the St. John's Wood
' Lane sheep-pens.

' I watered them freely with the pipe of the water-
' pot between the rows, when the pods were swelling
' and showing bloom; for if the plants lack moisture
' at this stage of their growth, when the weather is
' generally hot and the ground dry, the flowers seem
' to languish, and never attain that degree of perfec-
' tion they would do if the beds were kept moist and
' cool. The top-dressing prevents the ground from
' cracking, and the rains and water given from the
' pot passing through it, convey gradually a whole-
' some nourishment to the plants.

' The effect of careful, over careless cultivation, was
' never perhaps more clearly evinced than in an in-
' stance in my own neighbourhood in this season.
' A friend of mine, who had received from me all the
' superior varieties of Pinks, planted them in a bed
' in the common way; and though they were pretty
' healthy, and sent forth sufficient blooms, they pre-

' sented only a sort of uniform sameness, undistin-
' guished by that pleasing variety of bright colouring
' and beautiful lacing peculiar to each, which were
' so manifest in mine: a common observer would
' have said that they were Pinks altogether different
' from mine.

' Florists contending for a prize, and anxious to
' get their flowers large, leave three pods only upon
' each stem, and four or five stems to a large plant,
' two or three to a small one, cutting off the rest as
' they spindle up to flower: as soon as the pods are
' full formed they tie a slip of wet bass round them,
' to prevent their bursting irregularly, and place a
' glass or other covering over them when in bloom, to
' protect them from the sun and rain, thereby pre-
' serving their colours from being soon faded and
' tarnished.

' If there has been much frost during the winter,
' and the earth is consequently rendered light and
' loose when it thaws, the roots, by such an extension
' of ground, will sometimes be raised almost out of it:
' in that case it will be necessary, any time about the
' beginning of April, to tread the mould down lightly.

' with the foot, or at least to compress it firmly round
' the plants with the hand.

' A Pink bed will continue, and flower very well
' for two years in succession, though most florists
' renew their plants every year by piping the grass,
' in order to have them young, healthy, and vigorous;
' and if they are confined to the same plot of ground,
' they take care to add a little fresh loam and rotten
' dung to it, every time they make up a fresh bed.

' In preparing compost for the Dianthus tribe of
' plants, particularly for those which I flower in pots,
' I always bear in mind what Virgil says in his
' second Georgic about soil:—

> " Pinguis item quæ sit tellus, hoc denique pacto
> " Discimus; haud unquam manibus jactata fatiscit
> " Sed picis in morem ad digitos lentescit habendo."

' Columella and Pliny, also, in their works on Agri-
' culture, have given directions for the selection of
' good soil, which cannot be amended at the present
' day. The following are some of the tests whereby
' they distinguish it:—"That it is of a blackish
' colour: glutinous when wet, and easily crumbled
' when dry; has an agreeable smell; imbibes water,

' retains a proper quantity, and discharges a super-
' fluity," &c. Gardeners who cannot meet with such
' soil ought to use artificial means to form it, by
' bringing together different kinds: sand and stiff
' loam being the principal ingredients required, the
' one for strong soils, the other for light.

' Before I use fresh dung loam, I always take the
' precaution to strew over it a little quick lime, well
' slacked, and in a hot state, to correct any acidity, or
' decompose any injurious saline compounds. Lime
' also is an excellent application for the destruction of
' slugs, snails, worms, and other injurious insects, as
' well as for the dissolution of inert vegetable matter.

' You will excuse the minute detail, which I have
' entered into more fully than I intended when I sat
' down; but as I took the pains to make the experi-.
' ment, I give it you because I have every reason to
' be satisfied with the success of it.

' Before I conclude, I beg to call to your recollection
' that I am neither gardener nor florist professionally,
' but that I commenced the cultivation of flowers, in
' the first instance, with a view to amuse a depressed
' state of mind, and reinvigorate a still more sickly

' state of body: I therefore solicit your utmost indul-
' gence towards the remarks which I have made on
' the cultivation of that pleasing little flower the Pink.

  ' I am, Sir, with great respect,

   ' Your most obedient, humble Servant,

     ' THOMAS HOGG.

' *Paddington, July* 30, 1821.'

CATALOGUE OF THE PINKS.

IN the following catalogue I have taken the liberty
to discard the names of many of the old Pinks, and
which I mean in future to discard from the garden
also, because their places can now be much better
supplied with new ones; and if I have not published
a numerous list, let it be remembered that quality.
in respect to flowers, is always preferable to quantity

Archer's Seedling	Austin's Lady Hill
Ambrose's Lady Hill	——— Fair Ellen
——— King	——— No. 12.
——— Eclipse	——— Scarlett

Baker's King
Bennett's Woodstock Hero
Bray's Waterloo
Bond's Nelson
———— Stranger
———— Maid of Kent
Barnard's Bexley Hero
———— Mother Bunch
———— Curate
———— Miss O'Neil
Brooks' Superb
Barnes' Trafalgar
Berkshire Buffalo, or
   Beauty of Ugliness
Carpenter's Wellington
———— Blucher
Clay's Lady Nelson
Cheese's Miss Cheese
———— Champion
———— Caroline
Clarke's Smolensko
———— Leopold
———— Captain
———— Adonis
Cambray's Gibraltar
Colville's Eliza
Collin's Cornwallis
Corbett's Leopold
Chamberlaine's Bensonian

Chinn's Queen Caroline
Curson's Seedling
Coulston's Britannia
Collier's Kentish Hero
Davey's Britannia
———— Devonshire
———— Daveyana
———— Queen
———— Lady Shannon
———— Venus
———— Lady Durham
———— Eclipse
———— Agrippina
———— Lady Albemarle
———— Lady Bridgewater
———— Standard
———— Nonpareil
———— Hero
———— Incomparable
———— Miss Shutz
Dry's Earl of Uxbridge
Dakin's Burdett
East's Waterloo
———— Eclipse
Eggleston's Sovereign
Ford's King
———— Lady Hamilton
———— Queen Caroline
———— Mountain of Snow

Golding's Seedling
Green's Princess of Wales
Gould's Beauty
———— Windsor Hero
Greenwood's Britannia
———————— Beauty
Hopkins's Scarecrow
———————— Comet
———————— FarmerPickering
———————— Blucher
———————— Ruby
Harcourt's King George
Hine's Queen
———— Comet
———— Seedling 2
Hill's King
Hoare's Maid of Kent
Haslam's Parson Morris
———————— Ruler of England
Imber's Wellington
Jeeve's Glorioso
———————— Lady Dacre
Jeoffrey's Nelson
Knight's Wellington
Keen's Oldenburgh
Kilner's Cricketer
Langford's Burdett
———————— Countess of
  Pembroke

Looker's Oxonian
Lock's Glory of Newport
Lovegrove's Duchess of
  Gloucester
Maltby's Apollo
———— Adonis
Man's Duchess of Angou-
  lême
Metcalf's Blucher
Maynard's Rose-leafed
Moor's Seedling
Pope's Royal Purple
Pittman's Louisa
Picton's Ensign
Penning's Queen
Pottecary's Eclipse
———————— Queen
Perryn's Bright Scarlet
Rees' Eclipse
Sutton's Wellington
Sawyer's Archduke Charles
Style's Hero
———— Queen Caroline
Stevens' Fine Rose
———————— Waterloo
Spencer's Maria
Somerset Hero
Studwick's Blucher
———————— Duke of York

Smith's Windsor Castle
Thompson's Regent
Tagg's Wellington
Taylor's Lord Nelson
Turner's Regent
Princess Charlotte
Townshend's Trafalgar
Wollard's King George IV.
Wiltshire's Seedling
Wales's Beauty
Webb and Smith's Wellington

Willmer's Quiz
———— Little Henry
———— Illustrious
———— Coronation
———— Eclipse
———— King George IV.
———— Esquire Ricketts
———— Gamester
Watt's Sir William Watts
Weedon's Matchless
Williams' Queen Caroline

SCOTCH PINKS.

Buchanan's Caledonia
Dickson's Pomona
Finlayson's Bonny Lass
Henderson's Duchess of Athol
Johnson's Ossian
Martin's Isabella
Miln's Flora

Robertson's Gentle Shepherd
Stewart's Sir William Wallace
Sparke's Highlander
Wallace's Coat of Mail
———— Queen

OF THE AURICULA.

The Primula Auricula is a flower of great beauty, and in general estimation : it is not less remarkable for the great variety of its colours, than for their peculiar brightness. Its smooth broad leaf, of an oblong shape and glossy green, with an indented edge, sets off its polyanthus, or many-flowered blossom, to great advantage; each floret of which is supported by a small foot-stalk, rising from the top of the main stalk, the whole forming a magnificent bunch or truss, and exhibiting an appearance of grandeur but little suited to the size of the plant, or indeed expected from it; it flowers early in spring, and is, indeed, one of its greatest ornaments. Having but few rivals to contend with at that early period, it attracts our admiration the more, and seems to engross, in fact, our undivided attention. The scent which it diffuses is not powerful, but, like that of the Wild Primrose, is yet sweet and agreeable.

It is called an alpine or mountainous plant, because it is not only a native of the mountains, but
because it grows and thrives best in airy and elevated
situations. In low places, surrounded with damps
and fogs, it is difficult to keep it in any tolerable
health long together, or to get from it any very fine
bloom; whoever, therefore, attempts to grow Auriculas, living in such a situation, should keep them
during the winter in frames, raised at least two or
three feet above the level of the ground, and allow
them all the air possible, but a very scanty supply
of water during the three winter months. I am
induced to give this caution, because I know the
flower is so universally admired, that it is cultivated
in all places; and though art and culture may effect
a great deal, they cannot altogether change its nature
and habits.

The most prevailing colours of Auriculas are
brown and purple, of different shades, red, crimson,
rosy, violet, blue, yellow, &c. with white and yellow
eyes. They are divided into two classes—plain, or
self-coloured, and painted, or variegated; this last

G

consists of three sorts of varieties, which are distinguished from each other by the colour of the edges or margins of the petals, which is green, grey, and white.

The flowers are covered, more or less, with a species of farina or powder, which has a curious and pleasing effect, and serves, in some degree, to defend them against the rain and sun. This farina is not confined to the blossom only, but is scattered over the leaves of some plants, though not of all.

A fine green-edged Auricula may be briefly and simply described thus: — Every part must be in exact proportion one to another; the stalk must be proportionate to the leaves, and the pedicles and truss to them both; the prevailing or ground colour must be bright and distinct; the eye circular, and of a clear white; the border or edging round the petal of a lively green, and all the petals or pips nearly of a size, perfectly level, and disposed in regular order; the eye, the tube, and the rim, must correspond one with another, showing an exact symmetry throughout.

After this short account of the Auricula and its properties, I shall next proceed to point out the particular soil or compost in which it is found to thrive best.

In doing this, I am aware of the difficulty of giving any receipt, however excellent it may be, that will be generally approved or generally adopted; for the different composts used by florists in growing this flower are as numerous, I might say, as the florists themselves.

Almost all pride themselves in this, that they are in possession of some infallible nostrum, and some particular system, which are unknown to any but themselves; yet, after all this mystery and boasting, the state and condition of their plants too often belie their pretended skill, and expose their vain boasting, by showing that there is still great room for improvement.

Simple and easy methods of cultivation have always appeared to me most successful. I have often witnessed persons taking extraordinary pains, and incurring unnecessary expense, to injure, if not

destroy, their flowers, which they were so anxious
to preserve. Weak minds are soon misled by
quackery and novelty, having no sound judgment of
their own; and quackery, even in the growing of
flowers, has as many followers as in any other line.
By having recourse to hot manures, with the nature
and strength of which they are unacquainted, they
very often burn and poison, as it were, their plants
beyond all recovery, and learn experience only by
nearly the total destruction of their whole collection.

The late Matthew Kenney, gardener by profession, was, perhaps, one of the most successful and
eminent growers of Auriculas in his day, and won
as many prizes as most men, during the course of
ten or twelve years that he lived at Totteridge, in
Middlesex. He certainly had all the benefit of air,
situation, and soil, which, coupled with his fondness
for the flower, and his skilful treatment of it, to say
nothing of his being almost constantly in the garden,
gave him a decided superiority over many of his
competitors, and ensured, as it were, his chance of

success. He always kept by him a quantity of sound staple loam, of rather a sandy nature; this he sweetened by frequent turning. His next principal ingredient was sheep-dung and hay litter, well rotted, by being turned, mixed, and fermented in the same manner as the gardener does horse-dung and straw litter. This he never made use of under twelve or eighteen months, when it had the appearance of leaf or fine vegetable mould; sometimes he put to it a small portion of cow-dung, but this very seldom; a little clean coarse sand was generally added. These formed his compost for growing them in: but he had another of a richer quality, if I may so term it, with which he used to top-dress his plants, and this he would do sometimes twice in the year. When they killed any sheep, he always reserved the blood, and mixed it with the dung of poultry. These two ingredients he added to his loam and sheep-dung, and these constituted his compost for surface-dressing.

In fresh potting every year he trimmed and shortened the fibres, and reduced the roots with the

mould adhering to them to the bigness of a mode-
rate-sized ball, but never shook the mould completely from the roots, if they were sound and going
on well, until the third year; he then would wash
the roots in water, examine them closely, shorten
the tap or main root, and cut away any decayed
or unsound parts; but if any plant appeared
sickly at any time, he always served it in the same
manner.

He was particularly careful in making the holes
at the bottom of the pots larger, and putting in
three or four pieces of broken tile to drain the water
off, and prevent it from becoming stagnant at the
bottom of the pots: this, though apparently a trifling
circumstance, ought always to be well attended to.

The proportions he used, if I remember rightly,
(I speak only from memory,) were

$\frac{1}{3}$ Loam,
$\frac{2}{3}$ Sheep-dung and hay litter,
$\frac{1}{10}$ Coarse sand.

This sheep manure may be easily obtained from any
of the farmers about Finchley, or any other quarter,

who are in the habit of breeding and rearing house-lambs. Neat sheep-dung and loam only, would, I conceive, be of too close and heavy a nature for the Auricula.

Mr. Kennedy, the late partner of Mr. Lee, used this compost for their Auriculas, to whom Matthew Kenney disclosed its parts and mode of preparing it, and it was greatly approved of by him. Mr. Kennedy used to say that he did wonders with it, and that his flowers used to surprise everybody. He added, I understand, a small portion of leaf-mould, most likely from not always having the sheep-dung and litter in the proportions he wished. Sheep-dung is apt to breed a multitude of small white worms, which may easily be got rid of at any time by scattering over it a little quick-lime.

The compost in general use is as follows, and this I mostly make use of myself:—

$\frac{1}{4}$ Fresh yellow loam, or maiden mould,
$\frac{1}{4}$ Cow-dung, well rotten,
$\frac{1}{4}$ Night-soil, two years old,
$\frac{1}{4}$ Leaf-mould,
$\frac{1}{10}$ Sea or river sand.

To be well prepared and incorporated.

Auriculas grow very well in this mixture, which I conceive, upon the whole, a very good one; but they should be top-dressed about six weeks before they come into bloom, with compost of a stronger and more active manure. Emmerton's compost, of goose-dung and blood, night-soil, loam and sugar-bakers' scum, of each one-third, is well calculated for top-dressing in February.

Whoever grows Auriculas in low situations, will perhaps do well to use old frame-dung instead of cow-dung, because it dries sooner than cow-dung, which is better calculated for elevated situations. The circulation of air is always brisker on the hills than in vales; and, besides, I am inclined to attribute the rot, which in moist summers and autumns very frequently attacks the Auricula, to too great a portion of cow-dung in the compost.

Where a large stud of Auriculas (to use a Yorkshire term) is kept, it seldom happens that the same sort of compost precisely is made use of two years together; this is very often my case. I frequently, as opportunities occur, deposit in the same heap the dung of sheep, horses, cows, poultry, pigeons, night-soil, and blood from the slaughter-house, and turn and mix the whole up together.

The following compost is also excellent for strong blooming plants, and will retain its virtue for a length of time:

    1 Barrow of sound staple loam,
    1 Do. of dried night-soil,
    2 Do. of the dung of sheep, cows, and poultry,

mixed in blood from the slaughter-house, in equal quantities.

$\frac{1}{4}$ Do. of sea, or river sand, which will be fit for use in no case under two years.

MADDOCK'S AURICULA MOULD.

THE present edition of Maddock's Flower Directory, ' much improved,' published by Mr. Harding, St. James's Street, in which he has been assisted by a Mr. Samuel Curtis, lecturer on botany, contains the two following prescriptions, neither of which are ever likely to be made up by any experienced practical florists. The first, namely by Maddock, is too complex and difficult to be prepared by any one who is not conversant with fractional parts; it contains too much cow-dung by half.

$\frac{1}{2}$ Rotten cow-dung, two years old,
$\frac{1}{6}$ Sound earth of an open texture,
$\frac{1}{8}$ Earth of rotten leaves,
$\frac{1}{12}$ Coarse sea or river sand,
$\frac{1}{24}$ Soft decayed willow wood,
$\frac{1}{24}$ Peaty or moory earth,
$\frac{1}{24}$ Of the whole, ashes of burnt vegetables.

The second by S. Curtis, a theoretical florist, who considers loam unnecessary.

$\frac{2}{3}$ Rotten dung from hot-beds, reduced to mould,
$\frac{1}{3}$ Peat or bog-earth and sand in equal quantities.

It is well known to all the old florists, now living, that Mr. Maddock neither excelled in the culture of the Auricula, nor of the Carnation; but he managed Tulips and Ranunculuses well.

The 'much improved' in this edition, consists in a very extensive compilement of pirated extracts from Justice, Emmerton, and Hogg; and from the published Transactions of the London Horticultural Society, given by way of notes.

THE LANCASHIRE SYSTEM.

I HAVE had some conversation lately with a Lancashire florist concerning their mode of growing
them.   He told me that they were not half so particular as the London florists were, or at least as they
pretended to be.   It must be admitted that they are
entitled to great credit for the improvement they have
made in this class of flowers, as well as in that of the
Polyanthus ; they have undoubtedly in this respect
evinced much radical knowledge on the subject; we
are also chiefly indebted to them for most of our
finest gooseberries.   They use horse-dung and cow-
dung indiscriminately, sometimes mixed, sometimes
apart, the dung of poultry most frequently, and old
decayed willow wood, when they can get it, with the
mould cast up by moles, taking care that the same
be properly mixed, sweetened, and pulverized.

In winter they throw it up in narrow ridges, and
when the top of it is frozen, they take it off, and
so continue to do, till the whole of it has been frozen :

this is their principal preparation.   Very few of
them, especially the weavers, have frames and
lights, but they make use of weather-boarding with
hinges, fixed against some wall or fence, in a south
aspect, to defend them against the rain and snow,
resting, when shut close, upon a board nine inches
high ; but this is never done except in very severe
weather : the pots are plunged up to the rim in sand,
or coal-ashes; in blooming time they set their large
show plants under hand-glasses, in an east aspect,
to receive the morning sun only.   The plants are
perhaps not so early in bloom as those wintered in
frames, but then their stems are not drawn, and they
are able to support the trusses firmly ; the mildew
and rot do not take them so readily as when in closer
situations.

————

NOVEMBER, DECEMBER, AND JANUARY.

As my intention was, when I first set about this
small work, not to enter into all the minute history

of the Auricula, nor to follow it through every stage of its growth, and to state every trifling incident relative thereto, I will not depart now from such determination, but will proceed to give, in a summary way, a few general directions on all the points that appear to me most material and important.

I will resume the subject, then, with the commencement of the autumnal rains, which fall more or less towards the middle or end of October, and from which it is absolutely necessary to protect the Auricula, by placing it under cover. A temporary shelter for a few weeks longer would be infinitely preferable to placing them in their winter-quarters in the frames; but if you have no means of affording them this temporary shelter, put them at once into the frames, where they will have to remain till the spring. Let your frames be raised on a few bricks, to admit a free current of air under them, and so let them continue as long as the weather is open and temperate, which in some seasons is often the case till near Christmas. As soon as the frost sets in, remove the bricks, and let the frame rest on the ground. The plants will require, in all dry and temperate weather, to be exposed to the open air throughout the winter. Let them be set on four inches deep of coal-ashes, and be kept rather dry than otherwise till February, receiving the water you give them through the small pipe of a water-pot; be careful also not to let the water run into the heart of the plant, and contrive to give it them when the air is mild, and the wind southward. If the surface mould in the pots becomes incrusted from damp and stagnated air, the effect of too close confinement, take a small skewer, and stir the surface lightly, taking off at the same time any decayed leaves.

FEBRUARY AND MARCH.

WE will now suppose that we have reached the first or second week in February, and that the weather is open, with gentle rains occasionally; if that be the case, let the plants have the benefit of them for an hour or so, and this two or three times a week; and observe the same rule throughout March.

Any time in February when the weather permits, begin to top-dress your plants with some of your richest and strongest compost, as recommended before, removing first the mould from the top, without disturbing or injuring the fibres.

At the beginning of March, you may shift such of the plants as require it into larger pots to bloom; and as they begin to shoot up for bloom, reduce all the flowering stems to one, draw the lights off the greater part of the day, and give them all the air possible, to prevent the stems being drawn up weak, and let them receive all the gentle rains that fall from the middle to the end of this month, to encourage and promote their growth; but shut them close at nights, to prevent the opening blossoms being nipped by the frost, which will still frequently recur at this season.

It must be admitted that florists are indebted to Mr. Emmerton for the suggestion of extra covering by night, when the pips begin to open, to prevent

their receiving any sudden check or injury from
frost; and I hesitate not to say, that I have adopted
the use of a thick blanket, which I put next to the
glass, with a couple of stout mats over it, about the
20th of March, and continue it for three weeks or a
month, according as the weather may be; for it is
certain, that whatever petals are touched by frost
never become level nor show their right colours.

APRIL.

In this month the blossoms begin to expand and
display their rich and brilliant colours, and it is
then necessary to keep the lights over them night
and day, to preserve their beauty unimpaired, and
to admit air into the frame behind. The blossoms
must not only be protected from the rains, but also
from the mid-day sun, (which often begins about
this time to dart his fierce rays,) by a net or old
thin mat thrown over them. Notwithstanding this,
you must still shut them up close at night, and even

cover them with an additional mat, to prevent the blossoms being checked or injured by the frost. This is the very crisis of time that requires your most particular care.

As this flower produces more pips and blossoms than can expand at one time, it is necessary, at the beginning or so of this month, to cut out with great care the interior or middle pips, reserving not fewer than seven, nor more than thirteen : they should be taken out two or three at a time, and it requires some taste, nicety, and art, to perform this operation well, that the blossoms which are left may grow in a regular equidistant form, so that any common spectator might suppose that no such thinning of the pips had taken place, but that they had grown exactly in that form, and with that number, from the first.

By thus timely reducing the quantity of the pips, the rest are enabled to grow and increase greatly in size as well as beauty, and to give room to one another to expand, and become flat and level, which is a property required in all flowers that are exhibited for prizes.

To do this well, and bring the pips level, is a piece of art that the florist prides himself upon, and for which, as in the dressing of a Pink or Carnation, he takes to himself great praise.

Towards the end of this month, your flowers will have attained their greatest beauty and splendour: they should then be removed to the stage fronting the east, to catch the morning sun, which sun is all they require from this time till October.

I shall now leave you for a while to enjoy their smiles, contemplate their charms, and partake of their fragrance, with this strict injunction, that you do not keep them too long upon the stage, to the injury of their future health and well doing.

When you remove them from the stage, you must still continue them in a north-east aspect, to avoid the scorching rays of the summer's sun; they should be set upon thin boards or thin slates, lying on a bed of coal-ashes. Now they are out of bloom, they will require very frequent, almost daily watering, through the pipe of the water-pot, and occasionally with a fine rose, over the leaves. It is best to do this frequently and moderately, and not to saturate

them with too much water at one time. The decayed leaves should be taken off from time to time,
and the pots kept clear of weeds.

Owing to the continued rains that have fallen during
the last two autumns, (1818 and 1819,) and which
were too lasting and heavy for the plants to receive
and discharge without injury, I have been under the
necessity of erecting a covering of thin feather-edged
boards, which I fasten back or let down according to
the state of the weather; and I now place the plants
under it as soon as they are out of bloom, upon a
platform raised six inches above the ground, made
of deal, similar to those in green-houses; I have
found this a very convenient and appropriate situation; two hours of gentle rain are as much as they
ought to receive at any one time.

To encourage the growing of the seed, pluck the
withered blossoms from the seed-vessels; for if left
on, they are apt to retain the wet, and often injure
and prevent its ripening.

THE BEST TIME FOR FRESH POTTING CONSIDERED.

I AM now arrived at that part of my subject on which a great difference of opinion prevails amongst florists; namely, as to the proper time for fresh potting the plants. Many affirm, that as soon as the plants have performed their duty and flowered, and have relapsed into a state of comparative rest and inactivity, that is the only proper season to transplant and fresh pot them, which is towards the end of May. The off-sets are then to be taken off also. This is the season recommended both by Maddock and Emmerton, I, however, do not coincide in opinion with them, but approve of a later season for doing this, in which I am borne out by the practice of several, who do not perform this part of the business before the first week in August. The reasons which I have to offer are these : if you put your plants at this early period of the summer into pots, in which they are to remain till they flower again next spring, the space of nearly twelve

months, the strength of the compost must be greatly
reduced before that time, particularly as they require so much watering during the hot months of
June and July : this must tend, beyond all doubt,
to exhaust the nutriment contained in so small a
body of earth as is in the pots; by which means
they will be less able to throw out strong fibres, or
to produce you strong blooms in the spring.

This early potting is attended with another evil
consequence ; for, the plants being removed into
fresh and more vegetative earth, accompanied with
daily waterings, forces them prematurely into a state
of active vegetation, and causes them to flower late
in the autumn, a circumstance which the florist
always views with regret, as it in a great measure
destroys his hopes of a fine bloom at their natural
and expected season, towards the latter end of April :
this last argument of itself appears to me quite con-
clusive in favour of late potting.

The slips or off-sets will also have acquired more
strength and better roots, by being suffered to adhere
to the parent plant till the beginning of August, and

will occasion you less trouble in protecting and shading them.

From the beginning of August to the beginning of November, is a period quite long enough for the plants to strike fresh fibres, and to get well established in the pots, before winter; and, with the return of spring, you may expect a vigorous growth of the plant in all its parts.

The customary mode is, to shake the mould completely from the roots every second year; but, in doing this, you must be guided by the state and condition of your plants. ·Kenney, as I remarked before, lets his remain very frequently until the third year, reducing the ball of earth only, trimming the fibres, and examining the main root.

Transplanting should be done in a cloudy sky and a moist atmosphere.

In the former edition I gave a decided preference for late potting: I now beg to submit a few modifications of the above rule, which subsequent experience has suggested as necessary to be attended to. Whenever you perceive fresh roots issuing from the

neck of a plant above the mould, as is very often
the case during their quick growth in the spring,
such plant beyond a doubt ought to be fresh potted
the moment it has done flowering. I have no objection either to your fresh potting in May or June
such plants as you mean to shake completely from
the mould, for I have found plants so treated to take
twelve months to establish themselves again in the
pots; but those plants that you mean to remove
with a ball of earth to them, had better be deferred,
for the reasons above given, till the beginning of
August.

MODE OF TREATING FLOWERS WHICH ARE APT TO CUP.

SOME flowers, whose petals are of thick, firm texture, are generally inclined to cup, as Kenyon's
Ringleader, Bearlis's Superb, and several others;
when this is the case, they should be exposed a few
hours for two or three days in the very face of the
sun, under a hand-glass, shaded with a piece of

mat or gardener's blue apron. This warm confinement under the glass has the effect of gradually
producing a greater expansion of the petal, and of
making them pliable, so that with a little care and
nicety, and a thin piece of smooth wood, you will
be enabled to lock the edges of the pips under one
another and bring them level.

A piece of smooth ivory with a hole in it, nearly
the size of the pip, if pressed lightly upon the pip,
will also help to bring it level.

Plants that are in a forward state of bloom are
usually set under large hand-glasses upon bricks
during the day; and if they are not replaced in the
frames during the night, the bricks must be taken
away and a thick mat thrown over them. Great
benefit also arises from very lightly watering the
leaves of the Auricula when in flower, through a
very fine engine-turned brass rose, about the size of
half-a-crown, with a crane neck to prevent any water
falling on the blossom; this done about four o'clock
in the afternoon gives the leaves a lively and healthy
verdure in the morning: for it is well ascertained,

that plants not only draw through their leaves part of their nourishment, but that the leaves perform the necessary work of converting the water received at their roots into the nature and juices of the plants; hence it is that the lives of plants depend so immediately on their leaves.

RAISING OF PLANTS FROM SEED.

I HAVE already extended the subject of Auriculas farther than I intended: I will, therefore, conclude it with an observation or two respecting the raising of plants from seed.

Whatever seed you collect during the summer, keep it in a dry state till the time of sowing, which, if in the front part of a greenhouse, the best of all situations, should not be later than the 1st of February: by sowing then, you will be enabled to get your seedling plants into a forward state during summer, and may reckon on their blooming the following spring.

H

The seed should be sown in wide-topped 24-cast pots; the surface mould finely sifted, and made flat and even, and the seed not covered deeper than about the thickness of a crown-piece. Let the top be made level, and batted down after sowing with a smooth, flat board, or the bottom of a garden-pot.

As soon as the seed break ground, and the plants make their appearance, they should receive, almost daily, but at the same time very gentle, waterings, from a garden syringe or fine rose, to forward and encourage their growth.

If the seed is to be sown in the open air, let it be done in pans about the 1st of March, and a hand-glass kept over it to protect and forward it, and keep the rains from washing it bare. As soon as the plants will bear transplanting, remove them into wide-mouthed 48ths, and place them round the side of the pots, sheltering them from the hot rays of the sun. In the spring, shift them again into small pots of 60 to a cast, to bloom.

All pin-eyed flowers are accounted of no value, and may therefore be thrown away, as not worth the trouble of growing.

Considering the number of years that the Auricula
has been cultivated in this country, the varieties are
comparatively few; yet, from the increasing esta-
blishment of Flower Societies, not only in England,
but in Scotland and Ireland also,—in which Societies silver cups and other prizes are yearly awarded
to those members who exhibit the finest and most
perfect flowers,—and from the great pains and attention now paid to raising of seedlings, we may very
fairly expect, in the course of a few years more, a
very considerable accession of new flowers: indeed,
at this moment I know of several very superior seedlings in the hands of different florists; but it will be
some time before they can propagate such a stock of
each as shall induce them to put those new flowers
into circulation. They have also the ordeal of trial
to go through: they must win the first or second
prize at some exhibition or other, and have stood the
contest with some first-rate flowers. No common,
indifferent flower will be accepted. At no period, I
believe, has this flower been cultivated with so much
ardour as at present; and what will not perseverance

in any favourite pursuit accomplish? Some for their
amusement and gratification, some from motives of
gain, others again from a spirit of rivalship, and
many from a desire of fame, even in this pursuit,
and a wish to have their names registered in the
fancy-flower calendar, are anxious to produce new
varieties from seed, and, in truth, spare neither pains
nor expense to accomplish their desired object.

I have always found that young, vigorously growing plants of two or three years old, with only one
stem rising from the side, produce the roundest and
most perfect seed. Plants, then, of this age, and
possessed of good properties, both in respect to colour
and symmetry, ought to be selected for this purpose;
they should neither be kept too long in the frame nor
confined on the stage, but should have a full exposure to the air in a shady situation, yet receive the
morning rays of the sun; they, of course, must be
protected from· hail-storms and very heavy rains:
growing in this hardy state, they will undoubtedly
be more likely to ripen and perfect their seed.

The Auricula, like many other flowers, in its pro-

ductions from seed is inconstant, variable, changeful.
If you sow the seed of a green-edged flower, you
must not expect them to come all green-edged; nor
of a white-edged, all white-edged; indeed, you have
no right to expect they should come so, if the seed
has been saved from plants growing in the company
of all the sorts, for in that case the breed will undoubtedly be a mixed breed. To have a pure unmixed breed of clear, green-edged flowers, for instance,—as pure, at least, as the inconstancy of this
flower will admit,—it is necessary to remove two or
three plants of any one fine sort from the general
collection in the spring, before they come into flower,
to a distance, I would say, if it were possible, of a
mile, at least, from any other Auriculas: by doing
this, you will take all the reasonable pains, and use
all the feasible means, to ensure an unmixed breed;
you will prevent any impregnation; and if there be
a chance of the parent plant breeding an offspring
anything like itself, that chance will be yours.

I particularly press this upon the youthful florist;
as for the old humdrum, ignorant, conceited, blind

doodles, who do little, and noodles, who know little,
—why, let them pursue their own headstrong way.
'*Viam monstrare erranti*,' with such conjurors, is
time thrown away.

Pollit has lately raised a fine green-edged seedling
from his Highland Laddie upon this very principle,
which is now selling out under the name of Ruler of
England, and considered an excellent flower.

I am principally indebted to the ingenious Mr.
Warris, of Sheffield, a name well known among
florists, for the following minutely detailed method
of raising seedlings.

Every one who has made the experiment will, I
believe, admit with me, the difficulty which attends
the raising of Auriculas from seed.

The Auricula being among the earliest flowers of
the spring, it is requisite that its seed should be
sown almost with the commencement of the year, to
enable it to germ, vegetate, and grow precisely at
that season which Nature has assigned for the principal growth of this plant. If you defer sowing till
the middle of March, or beginning of April, the

young plants will hardly make their appearance before May, when the Auricula has nearly done both
growing and flowering, and is relapsing into a state
of inactivity; thus they will lose that particular
impulse of nature, which would so materially promote their growth and progress. If great care be
not taken in watering and shading at this late season,
it is very great chance indeed but they are scorched
and burnt up by the sun. Let your seed be sown
early in January, at any rate not later than the first
of February, in pots adapted to the size of your
striking or bell glasses, no matter whether in 32 or
24-sized pots, which are to be filled one inch and a
half deep at the bottom with broken oyster-shells,
tiles, or small cinders, to ensure a good drainage;
then fill the pots with finely-sifted compost, and
smooth the top of it with a flat smooth board, made
round to fit the inside of the pot; let the compost be
fullest in the middle, gradually falling to the sides
of the pot. Then sow your seed as regularly as you
possibly can, and cover it, as near as you can guess,
with fine mould passed through a sieve to the thick-

ness of a shilling: take a clothes or other soft brush
and dip it into soft water, giving it a shake to throw
off the heavy weight of the water, then either shake
it over the seed, or draw your hand along the hair,
and it will fall like a dew upon it; repeat this till you
perceive the compost to be well moistened. By
watering in this manner you will not be liable to disturb or wash out the seed.

You may then put on the bell-glasses, or if you
have not these, you may cover the seed with squares
of window-glass, resting on the tops of the pots,
which, in the opinion of many, answer full as well,
if not better. Place the pots in pans or saucers in
the front of a greenhouse, or the window of a dwell-
ing-house close to the glass, where they will have
the benefit of the sun, and keep the saucers well
supplied with water, so as to render top-watering
less frequent and necessary. If you perceive at any
time a little mouldiness on the surface of the mould,
arising from the confined damp, take off the glasses
for a day, and let them be wiped and dry before you
replace them.

The seed, if good, and kept moist, and the wea-ther prove favorable, will strike root and make its appearance in a month, but sometimes not under six weeks. When the seed is up, I then recommend you to take away the striking glasses, and place squares of window-glass over the pots in their stead, for you must be careful not to confine them too long, and so draw them up weak, as you would mustard and cress. Give air gradually, and harden them to it by degrees. The young plants, when beginning to sprout, will sometimes throw their roots out of ground, which must be carefully put in again, by making a small cleft in the earth, and closing the soil round them; this may be done with a long flat bit of ivory or smooth wood, thin at the end, and about one-eighth of an inch broad, or they will come to nothing.

As soon as the plants are fit to handle, transplant them carefully into store pans or pots, an inch apart, filled with proper compost, which ought to be raised in a convex form, one inch and a half higher in the middle than at the sides; water with the brush as

before, and place the flat window-glass over the tops
of the pots, for a week or two longer, shading them
from the sun in the middle of the day. Water as
often as you see occasion. If your plants thrive and
do well, in a month or five weeks more you may
transplant them a second time into fresh compost,
which will very much encourage their growth, where
they may remain till August, when you may plant
them singly in 60-cast pots, or put three round the
edge of a 48, for next spring bloom.

'Non omnia possumus omnes.'—VIRGIL.

Yet I am satisfied if you pursue the mode which
I have laid down, you will succeed, and there is certainly more pleasure in rearing and nursing a handsome bantling of your own, than in adopting that of
another, even though it should be gifted with superior charms.

SYMPTOMS OF DISEASE IN AURICULAS.

ANY time in the year when you perceive an Auricula grow crooked, and throw its top or head on one
side, like a hen with the pip, as an old gardener
once observed, it is evident disease has commenced :
the plant must be taken up immediately if you wish
to save it, and be carefully examined. The roots
ought to be washed, and every unsound part cut
away. Cracks in the side are indicative of decay.
A purplish hue at the bottom of the leaves and
round the neck, denotes danger of mortification.
When plants have been removed into fresh compost
for some time, and begin to look sulky and sickly,
and make no progress, you may take it for granted
that they dislike their food : remove them again into
a simple compost of fresh sweet loam, sand, and leaf
mould, till they recover their verdure.

Incautious watering in the heart or cup formed by
the leaves will often occasion decay, particularly in
winter, when there is neither wind to dry, nor sun

to exhale; it will remain for two or three days before it be all imbibed.   Any pot that does not dry readily like the rest will soon become sickly from the stagnation of water; proper drainage is wanting. Sick plants should be removed and set by themselves. The diseases among Auriculas are said to be often infectious, and will sweep off a whole collection in the course of a few weeks; this shows that care and attention are always required.

Archer's Champion
Ashworth's Rule All
Barlow's Morning Star
Bearless's Superb
Booth's Freedom
Butterworth's Lord Hood
——————— Duchess of
  Wellington
Brown's Mrs. Clarke
Barlow's King
Buckley's Jolly Tar
Clegg's Lady of Honour
——————— Black and Green
——————— Blucher
Clough's Do-little
——————— Defiance

Cox's British Hero
Chilcott's King
——————— Brilliant
Crompton's Adm^l. Gardner
Coldham's Blucher
Dean's Smoker
——————— Regulator
Dyson's Queen
Eaton's Volunteer
Eggleton's Alexander
Foden's Victory
——————— Rosamond
Grimes's Privateer
——————— Hyder Ali
Gorton's Champion
Goldham's Vertumnus

Hayley's Prince of Wales

Hey's Lovely Ann

Hoffley's or Howard's Lord Nelson

Hughes's Pillar of Beauty

Kenyon's Ringleader

Leigh's Colonel Taylor

—— Talavera

Lee's Venus

—— Sir William Wallace

Lawrie's Glory of Cheshunt

—— Field Marshal

Metcalf's Hero

Moore's Jubilee

—— Marchioness of Salisbury

Ogden's Sir Rowland Hill

Owen's Princess of Wales

Pollit's Highland Boy

—— Ruler of England

Page's Oldenburgh

—— Champion

—— Waterloo

Pott's Regulator

—— Delegate

Pearson's Badajoz

Partington's Sir Solomon

—— Trafalgar

Pendleton's Violet

Popplewell's Conqueror

Rider's Waterloo

Scholes's Mrs. Clarke

Snook's Beauty

—— Regulator

Slater's Cheshire Hero

Stretch's Alexander

—— Waterloo

Smith's Emperor

—— Duke of Sussex

—— Waterloo

Simpson's Marquis of Granby

Tomlinson's Commander-in-chief

Thompson's Bang-up

—— Revenge

Tranter's Constellation

Thornicroft's Invincible

Taylor's Ploughboy

—— Glory

—— Incomparable

—— Victory

—— Alexander

Warris's Blucher

—— Union

—— Colossus

Whitehead's Reform
Waterhouse's Seedling
Wrigley's Northern Hero
Wild's Colonel Anson
——— Lord Cochrane

Wild's Lord Bridport
——— Highland Lass
——— Black and Clear
Wood's Lord Lascelles
Yates's Collingwood

PLAIN OR SELF-COLOURED OF VARIOUS SHADES.

Redman's Metropolitan
Hey's Apollo
Bury's Lord Primate
Schole's Ned Ludd
Whittaker's True Blue
Howe's Venus
Hogg's Urania

Webb's Caroline
Howe's Cupid
Flora's Flag
Lee's Mrs. Munday
Ancient Lady
Grand Turk,
&c. &c.

POLYANTHUS.

Pub: by Whittaker Treacher & C.º Ave Maria Lane.

A. Ducôtes Lithog.º 70 S.ᵗ Martins Lane

OF THE

PRIMROSE AND POLYANTHUS.

The Polyanthus, in its culture, bears the same relation to the Auricula as the Pink does to the Carnation; differing, however, in this respect, like the Pink, that it is hardier in its nature, and more easily cultivated.

Though all plants appear to grow in nearly the same manner, and the same sort of earth or soil to suit the same kind and species, and though their common parts and constituent principles are proved by a chemical analysis to consist of similar materials, yet their colours, tastes, and scents, are as various as their forms, and bear no analogy or resemblance to each other.

The Primrose and Polyanthus require a much greater portion of sandy loam than the auricula, a very small quantity of rotten cow-dung, and a little leaf-mould or heath or peat earth, mixed with them:

in this they are found to grow extremely well. The double paper-white Primrose requires no dung at all, indeed dung is hurtful to it.

The Double Primrose is truly a beautiful flower; the different coloured sorts of which are:—

White,	Pink,
Yellow,	Crimson,
Lilac,	Purple.

It is propagated by off-sets from the root, which may be parted as soon as it is done flowering.

The Polyanthus consists of many different tints and shades; but the most esteemed are, a bright red or scarlet, and a very dark crimson, and chocolate with brimstone or lemon-coloured eyes, and the edging of the same.

Let it be remembered, that those flowers, if planted in the ground, and which indeed is the only successful way of growing them, should be in a situation exposed to the morning rays of the sun, and excluded from them the rest of the day. It is folly, and a waste both of time and plants, to keep them all the year round in pots, especially in the near vicinity of London: I have found it so; others may, perhaps, be more successful. I admit it is convenient to have them in pots in the spring, both for exhibition and sale: in this case, the moment the pips begin to fade, turn them into the ground, and let them remain there till near Michaelmas, when you may again remove them into pots. Keep slugs. and snails from them. The Polyanthus in coming into flower should be set under a hand-glass raised upon bricks, and shaded; constant exposure to the air soon tans the bright lemon-coloured eye and lacing.

Bray's Wellington
Buck's Traveller
Billington's Beauty of Over
Brown's King
Cox's Regent
Crownshaw's Invincible
Darlington's Defiance
Fletcher's Defiance
Fillingham's Tantararara
Hattersley's Invincible
Harley's Sceptre
—— Defiance

Heapey's Smiler
Hopkins' King
Johnson's Miss Mitford
Lombard's Highlander
Lee's Magnificent
—— Superb
—— Harlequin
Mason's Black Prince
Massey's Venus
Martin's Prince William
Moore's King
Parke's Lord Nelson

Pearson's Alexander
——— Blackguard
——— Defiance
Radcliff's Waterloo
Steed's Telegraph
Stretch's Traveller
Thomas's Invincible
——— Waterloo
Turner's Buonaparte
——— Prince of Wales
——— Princess
——— Marquis of Titch-
field

Tandy's Blucher
——— Regent
Thomas's Ruler of Eng.
land
Thompson's Lord Nelson
Thorpe's Golden Ball
Wilde's Gleaner
Waterhouse's Incompa-
rable
——————— Princess
Charlotte
Warris's Alderman Wood
Yorkshire Regent

Note.—Mason's Black Prince and Turner's Marquis of Titchfield, lately raised from seed, are both fine flowers.

OF THE RANUNCULUS.

———

THE Ranunculus Asiaticus, or Garden Ranunculus, is a flower very generally, but at the same time very unsuccessfully cultivated: it is very seldom indeed that you have an opportunity of beholding this flower in any great perfection; but if you are fortunate enough to meet with a bed of the choicest sorts, growing in full health and vigour, and bearing a profusion of splendid blossoms of all colours, plain and variegated, you will be forced to admit that it is an admirable sight, and one of the grandest displays of nature in vegetable life. A bed of fine Ranunculuses is esteemed by many in no degree inferior to a bed of the richest Tulips.

Here yellow globular blossoms present themselves in all shades, from the pale straw to the golden crocus; red of all tints—pink, rose, and flame colour; purple and crimson of every dye; black, brown, olive, and violet, of every hue. Besides these, there are yellow-spotted flowers, brown-spotted, and white-spotted, red and purple streaked, red and white striped, red and yellow striped, besides mottled and brindled in countless varieties.

I have had occasion to remark more than once, when purchasing Ranunculus roots of a very eminent seedsman and florist in Fleet-street, that when I inquired of him what kind of soil was best calculated for them, he answered, a strong loamy soil without dung. I have proved the fallacy of such an observation. That they will grow in it is true, but in a very stunted, starved, and imperfect state, with stems weak and short, and blossoms small and insignificant. That fresh loamy soil is proper I admit, but then it is necessary to add a considerable portion of rotten horse or cow dung.

Your choice Ranunculus roots should never be planted in our variable climate before the middle of February, or the beginning of March, as the weather may be.

It is true, they will live in the ground through a tolerably mild winter without much covering, and sustain no injury, and most likely will blossom earlier by being planted in October: but is it worth the while to run that risk, or endanger the safety of a rare and valuable collection, that has required no small trouble and expense to get together? Prudence forbids it.

Treading the ground close round the plants, as soon as they have made their appearance in the spring, to keep the cold winds from cracking the ground and injuring the roots, is, I conceive, a very unwise and improper step, for the fibres must be bruised and injured by it. The better mode is to top-dress the bed with an inch thick of old cow-dung: this will protect them, and at the same time keep the bed moist and cool afterwards, when the sun shall have acquired greater power, and rendered watering necessary.

An old book has just been put into my hand, called the ' Complete Florist,' written above a hundred years ago, by Henry Van Oosten, a Dutch gardener at Leyden. In treating of the Ranunculus, he writes thus :—

' This flower is admired for its beautiful and
' lively colours, which dazzle the sight when the sun
' shines upon them. It must be planted the latter
' end of October, in good loamy soil, that has been
' well dunged before. Dig the ground above a spit
' deep where you intend to make the bed, and throw
' it out on each side, then put in near a foot thick of
' horse-dung, half rotten, that has not yet lost all its
' strength; upon this lay the earth you had taken
' out before, but let it be well worked and broken to
' pieces first: it should be often turned in the sum-
' mer. Plant the roots two inches deep, and four
' inches apart every way; when this is done, lay on
' the top of the bed night-soil an inch thick, quite
' reduced to mould. He that has none, may use
' horse-dung in the same manner.'

The making of your bed I would recommend to
be done in this way: let the depth of your mould
be nearly two feet, and the whole of that depth
turned and dug. The calculation, I believe, is
pretty accurate, when I say, that the length of the
roots or fibres of any tree or plant is in proportion to

their height, and therefore the small stringy fibres of the Ranunculus will nearly reach to that depth.

If your loam is fresh and without manure, after having dug it, put towards the autumn all over the surface of the bed six or eight inches deep of rotten dung from some cucumber pits, and there let it remain for two months, after which, dig or trench it in a foot deep; your bed will then be ready for planting in the spring; and if your loam is not well worked, throw the surface mould into small ridges in the winter, so that the frost may have greater power to act upon it; for frost, after all, is one of Nature's best workmen in preparing soils for vegetation, crumbling the hardest clods to powder. In a bed so constructed, you may plant your Ranunculus roots for three successive years, giving it every autumn a similar dressing of manure: after that time you must give them a fresh situation, or some fresh soil in the garden.

Almost all flowers confined too long to the same earth and same spot, I was going to say, and to the same air, degenerate and dwindle away: a change in all three respects is often requisite, to renovate, as it were, their crescive faculties, and to ensure their return to their pristine health and condition. Should it be found inconvenient to prepare a bed of fresh soil, and you are under the necessity of planting them in the common garden mould, in this case, if the mould be light and porous, it will then be requisite that you put a stratum of loamy soil six inches deep, to set the roots in. This will help to retain a greater degree of moisture, and serve also to protect them from the searching rays of the sun; for they ought never to be planted deeper in the ground than an inch and a half; if set deeper, they exhaust their strength in forming a fresh root exactly at that depth, and of course neither flower well, nor yield any good increase.

The readiest and most certain mode of planting is by drawing drills along the bed, exactly two inches in depth, and then scattering a little coarse sea or river sand along them: in these set the roots, with the claws downwards, and press them gently into the sand. If the breadth of your bed be four feet, and the roots large and good, you may divide it into six rows, and set the roots four inches apart. In covering, be careful not to displace them, and let them be buried as near an inch and a half as possible: you may then take the flat side of the spade, and beat down the surface level: this will in some measure prevent the worms from casting them out. Let it be remembered, that the bed is to be perfectly level and even, that it may receive all the rain or water in an equal proportion.

As soon as they shoot up for bloom, if the weather should be dry, they will require an abundant supply of soft water, to encourage a quick growth. I am at a loss to know why the ancients have given to this flower the name of Ranunculus, or Frog-plant, unless it be meant to imply that during the time of its flowering it delights in a plentiful supply of water, which must be given between the rows, and not over the blossoms. The tints of those flowers, particularly the darker sorts, are so fine and delicate, that they soon get tarnished and fade, if they are not sheltered from the scorching rays of the sun. The duration

I

of this flower is nearly a month, if you take but the pains to shade them.

By the middle of July the stems will have become withered and decayed, which points out the time for their being taken up : this should be done on a dry day. The stems may be shortened, but not cut close to the roots yet; and the roots should be parted before they get dry and hard, or else they are apt to break in parting. Let them be dried gradually in a shady room, open to a free circulation of air.

The Anemone may be treated in every respect as the Ranunculus, with this slight difference, that it requires to be planted a little deeper in the ground: to say more would only be an unnecessary repetition of the same directions.

Many persons are fond of buying Dutch Ranunculuses and Tulips, which now come over every autumn, under the impression of not only getting them very cheap, (which, of course, they sometimes are enabled to do, as it would not answer the importer's purpose to send them back again to Holland unsold,) but also of getting them very fine. In this

they are not very seldom disappointed; for the
Dutchman is something like the Jew in his dealing.
You must not expect great bargains for little money:
he is very seldom charged, I believe, with sending
us any of his best flowers among his common mix-
tures; his Pell-mells, as the florist calls them, are,,
upon the whole, very indifferent, and not worth the
amateur's notice.

This tribe of named flowers is so very numerous,
that to give a list of their names would occupy more
space than I can allow them in this short treatise; I
will therefore only add the names of a few of them.

Catalogue of Ranunculuses.

Abbé St. André	Bon Chrétien
Ajax	Berenice
Agloe	La Chabonniere
Arcadia	Cassandra
Arlequin	Cedo nulli
Aurora	Clorinde
Beauté des Dames	Daphne
—— Parfaite	Diana
Beau Regard	Doris
Bishop of Lima	Don Quivedo
Belle Capuchine	Diadème Pourpre

Drusilla
Diagoras
Emma
Euphrates
Evêque de Bruges
Feu de Fontenoy
Feu Granade
Fanor
Favorite Mignonne
Faventella
Fabian
Fulgor Solis
Grand Berger
Grand Monarque
Hecate
L'Impératrice
Le Mélange des Beautés
La Médaille
Marmara
Miriam
Manteau Royal
Naxara
Nègre
Niobe
L'Œil Noir
Le Nègre Superbe
Œillet Bizarre
Plato
La Princesse Charmante
Pizarro

Passe Brutus
Paris
Quixos
Rodney
Roi Rouge
Roxana
Rose Incomparable
Rose of Sharon
Rose Monstrueuse
Sarah
Sophia
Sappho
Thais
Téméraire
Totilla
Terentius
Venus
Virgo
Vesta
Violet Bleuâtre
———— Superbe
Violà le vrai Noir
Vereâtre
Vulcan
La Zébra
Zoile
Zephyr
Zagoras
Zaire

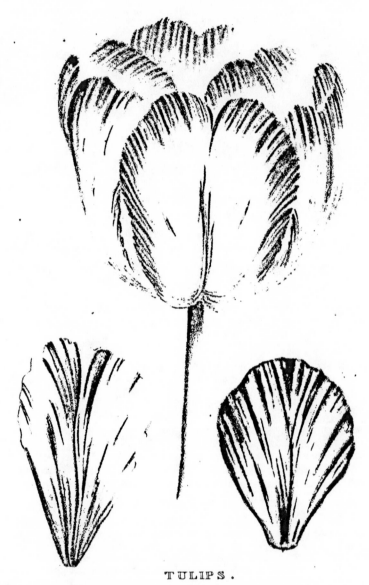

TULIPS.

Pub. by Whittaker Treacher & Cº Ave Maria Lane

OF THE TULIP.

If the account which I here give of the Tulip be short and defective, I trust the following apology will be considered satisfactory. I had, indeed, purposed, at setting out, to pass it over altogether, not only because I was unwilling to swell this treatise to a size that might render it inconvenient to be carried in the pocket, as a kind of manual, which the florist might readily and easily consult, and for which I intended it, but because those flowers (I mean the finer sorts) are not so very generally cultivated. I have since, however, been induced to change my determination; and, in doing so, shall confine the subject matter to those points more essentially and more immediately relating to its cultivation: by this, I shall perhaps avoid the reprehensions, in some measure, of all those whose attention is almost exclusively directed to the culture of this flower, and who consider every other as unworthy of their notice. To such I can with truth say, that I have always been a great admirer of the Tulip, and that I esteem it the masterpiece of perfection, and one of the greatest ornaments of the garden. Many a poor florist may be justly lavish in its praise, without ever having it in his power to gratify his wish with the possession of it. A moderate collection of choice Tulips,—of those beautiful, those exquisitely beautiful flowers, which are the pride and boast of every amateur who grows them, could not be purchased for a sum much less than one thousand pounds, at the usual catalogue prices, nor obtained and got together till after years of patient search and unwearied labour.

The high prices that have for many years been affixed to Tulips in the printed catalogues of our florists are so deterring and repulsive of the fancy, that persons with a taste and fondness for this flower are afraid to indulge and enter into it. Those prices are generally rated nearly one-half higher than they may be bought at, both here and in Holland; this has a bad effect, and wears the appearance of imposition, and beyond doubt prevents a more extensive culture of them.

The Tulip, according to Gesner, is a native of Cappadocia, a province of Natolia, or Asia Minor, though some others affirm that it grew spontaneously, and was common to most of the islands in the Levant, or Eastern Mediterranean Sea. It was introduced into England in the year 1577, where it has been found to increase freely, and to grow in the open ground without any extraordinary degree of care.

We are indebted to this part of the world both for some of our choicest fruits as well as flowers—as, for instance, apples, cherries, peaches, plums, quinces, and some peculiar sorts of grapes. We have received from thence some of our most beautiful lilies and irises; for what is finer than the white lily and the scarlet martagon, or more curious than the Iris Susiana? The musk and damask roses, and the greater part of odoriferous shrubs, were brought from thence.

The inconstancy of the seed of the Tulip has mul-

tiplied its varieties beyond all calculation, though a
bulb raised from seed will hardly ever break into its
true colours under seven years; he, therefore, that
wishes to add to that variety, has many years to wait
of patient, though anxious expectation, before his
wish can be gratified.

The fresh spirit that has been infused into the
cultivators of flowers, since our return to peace and
to peaceful pursuits, has induced many to try to raise
a fresh set of breeders, and to sow seed annually that
has been saved from fine flowers. The enthusiastic
florist overlooks every difficulty; eager with hope,
and ardent in the pursuit, he anticipates success,
and his perseverance effects it. After three years of
application, he will nearly have accomplished his
object: he will then have a succession of bulbs, and
be gratified every succeeding year with the appearance of bloom, and the production of new varieties
as they break into colour. The most gratifying and
complete success has attended the labours of Mr.
Carter, of Foxgrove, Wiltshire; of a Mr. Austen, a
Mr. Strong, a Mr. Lawrence, and a Mr. Goldham,

who have raised from seed, and matured and broke
into colour, perhaps some of the finest Tulips in the
country. Mr. Clarke, of Croydon, a scientific and
experienced florist, has the best breeders in the kingdom, raised from the seed of Louis, Charbonniere,
Davey's Trafalgar, &c., with finely-formed cups and
clear bottoms; they are in very high repute among
florists. Let others persevere, and they will have
the same success. No great skill or art is required;
time, patience, and perseverance are alone wanting.

Mr. Clarke's mode of sowing the seed is as follows:—

The best time for sowing the Tulip seed is the
latter end of January, or the beginning of February,
and in pots used for Carnations. Let the earth be
good, and put some lime-core at the bottom of the
pot, or the plants will be destroyed by the worm,
&c. &c. Cover the seed half an inch, and keep the
earth moist. When sown, put the pots under a light,
and keep them from severe frost. When the plants
are up, the pots may be set out, so as to have the
sun; but when the sun becomes powerful, they

should be set so that they may have the morning
and evening sun only.   Keep the plants in a growing state by watering occasionally, till the leaves are
entirely dead.   Let the pots be then kept dry for a
time, and then take up the small bulbs and dry them
gradually as usual.   The first time of planting them
may be the middle of October, or a little earlier, in
the open ground, and little more than two inches
deep.

The Tulip is generally divided into two classes—
the early dwarf and the taller late flowering; and
both are further distinguished according to their tints
and their peculiar mixture—as Flakes, Bibloemens,
Bizarres, Rigauts, Baguets, &c., on grounds both of
white and yellow.

To describe their different and variegated colours
would be a work almost impossible; I shall, therefore, proceed to point out the soil most suitable for
them, and the time and manner of planting.   We
will suppose the bed is intended for your best sorts,
which must be situated in an open part of the garden.   The earth most proper for it is a fresh and

rich loamy soil, of rather a sandy nature, which should be dug twelve months, at least, before it is used. Many florists are afraid of adding dung, lest it should start the colours, and render the cups foul, and therefore use none; but if you wish to blow them of any size, you must, however, add a small portion, taking care that it be well rotten and incorporated with the loam. Perhaps the safest way, after all, is to dig a little dung in at the bottom of the bed, a foot, at least, below the bulbs.

A very intelligent and old Tulip grower assured me, that the best compost he could ever hit upon, after many experiments, was the following; the component parts of which were:

$\frac{3}{4}$ Rich yellow loam,
$\frac{1}{x}$ Leaf mould,
$\frac{1}{6}$ Two year old horse-dung,
$\frac{1}{8}$ Sea sand.

The bed was dug two feet deep.

The usual time of planting them, according to the ' Florist's Calendar,' near London, is the Lord Mayor's Day, which is the 9th of November: the distance between the rows should be nine inches, and from bulb to bulb in the row seven, the depth four.

After the bed is lined and marked out, the most simple method of planting them is, to get a blunted dibber, with a circular mark round it, or a nail driven in it, at the distance of about five inches from the end, which will direct you how deep you are to make the holes, into each of which you are to put a little sea or river sand, before you set the bulbs in; this helps to keep them dry in the winter, as the rain-water passes through it, and improves likewise their coat or external skin. It is not customary to give them water in any stage of their growth; as soon as they are out of flower, break off the seed cup, to encourage the growth of the bulb.

Van Oosten, whom I mentioned before, says, ' The florist who wishes to observe proper arrange-
' ment of height, and a pleasing mixture and variety
' in the bed, should have a box of convenient length
' and breadth, to put as many tulips in as his bed will
' contain, and this box must be divided into as many
' compartments as bulbs; which are to be put in the

'same order in the box as they are to be set 'in the bed; and when they are taken up, to be 'replaced in the box as before.' This plan is at once simple and convenient, and I believe generally adopted. The bulbs, he says, must be taken up every year, or they will degenerate and come to nothing; and if transplanted every year into fresh ground, that has been turned three or four times, they are the better for it in every respect.

Persons who have valuable collections are in the habit of hooping them over in very wet and in very sharp frosty weather, and of covering them during such periods with mats, yet avail themselves of every opportunity to give air. Heavy hail-storms in particular must be guarded against. The same precaution against bleak, chilling easterly winds in February and March ought to be adopted as is recommended by the Dutch florist in the treatment of his Hyacinths at the same season. Those winds chill and stagnate the sap, arrest the progress of vegetation, and do infinite mischief every way.

To bloom Tulips in perfection, an erection ought

to be raised over them, and covered with stout Scotch sheeting, reaching to the ground, to be drawn up and let down with pulleys : by doing this you may keep them in high condition for three weeks, during which time you will have a full opportunity of gratifying your friends with a view; for the true enjoyment of every pleasure is to share it with them.

I conceive it unnecessary to mention, that if you wish to preserve the beauty of their blossoms, you must protect them against the sun, rain, and wind; at the same time, you must allow them all the air possible, lest the stems be drawn up weak, and so rendered unable to support the cups.

The careful florist frequently runs a small cord along the rows, and fastens the stems to it, just below the cup, with green-coloured worsted: this has no unpleasant appearance.

The bulbs must be taken up every year; for, if they are suffered to remain two years together in the ground, they become foul, and break into small increase, so that it will be two or three years before they can recover their size, and produce any good blossoms.

As soon as the stems are nearly withered away, take up the bulbs on a cloudy day, place them in shallow wooden boxes, or on boarded floors, to dry, and let them have sun and air. Brick or stone floors are fatal to them; they will contract a dampness, and a mildew that will destroy them. Let them be arranged singly, and not one upon another. I have seen a quantity of common Tulips thrown into a hamper with a lid over when taken up, and in forty-eight hours they have heated and rotted, and bred maggots.

After the fibres are completely withered, rub them off gently, and pluck the dead stem from the bulb; then put them away in some dry place till the planting season again comes round. These are all the directions which I conceive necessary for the culture of the Tulip.

*The following short Catalogue contains a few of
the most valuable Sorts.*

ROSE-COLOURED TULIPS.

Andromeda
Altesse
Amaryllis
Amadis
Bathsheba
Bacchus
Beeterer Brûlante
——— Eclatante
La Brûlante Eclatante
Buisson Ardent
Claudiana
Comte de Vergennes
Cerise Supérieure
—— Palmyre
—— Eudonie
——— Lambelle
Clio
Calista
Daviana
Elizabeth
Henriette
Impériale
Juno

Lord Colchester
Lavinia
Madame Catalani
Maria Theresa
Maria Louisa
Manon
Matilda
Minerva
Mercurius
Nannette-
Ponceau Unique
——— Très-Blond
Reine des Cerises
Roi des Cerises
—— de Roses
Rose Cerise Blanche
—— Brillante
—— Camuse de Craix
—— Camuse
—— Primo Bien du Noir
—— Esther
—— William
—— Première

Rose Primo
—— Hebe
—— Triomphe Royal
—— Thalestris
Surpasse Ponceau Très-
    Blond

Surpasse Thalestris
La Tendresse
Toilette de la Reine
Vesta
Walworth

BIBLOEMEN.

Ambassadeur d'Hollande
Acapulca
Amiable Brunette
Abbé de St. Michel
Belle Actrice
Blue Violet
Chaumont
Clarke's Euphrosyne
Comte de Saxe
Clitus
Constantia
Cramoisi Superb
Duc de Florence
Duchess of Wellington
Directeur-Général
David
Duchess of Clarence
Endymion
Imperatrix Florum
Franciscus Primus

Gloria Alborum
Grotius
Holmes's King
Josephine
Louis XVI.
Lysander
L'Impératrice de Maroc
Leonard
La Belle Duchesse de
    Parma
La Mère Brune Incompa-
    rable
La Charbonniere
Cornwallis
Lysander Noir
Majestueuse
Magnifique
Prince Souverain
Princess Charlotte's Ceno-
    taph

Perle Blanche
Prince de Condé
Roi de Siam
Reine de Violets
—— de Sheba
—— de Fleurs
Rubens
Sang de Bœuf

Superbe en Noir
Scipio
Selina
Transparent Noir
Violet Alexandre
———— Superbe
Washington

BIZARRES.

Ariadne
Alfred
Abercrombie
Brutus
Buonaparte
Bugby's Hector
Bizarre Eclatante
Commander-in-Chief
Captain White
Cenotaph
Charbonnier Extra
Cimon
Count Platoff
Castrum Doloris
Catafalque (Old Dutch)
———————— Superbe
Davey's Trafalgar
Duke of York

Etna
Eucharis
Earl Chatham
Feu en Feu
Godfrey's Sir Vincent
Gloria Mundi
Groland
Hector
Holmes's Regent
Heroine
Leopoldina
Louisa
Laurence's Duke of Clarence
Lord Hill
Lord Wellington
Pluto
Polyhymnia

Milo
Mon Amie
Mizraim
Masonia
Merveille d'Europe
Necker
Nicanor
Nonpareille
Optimus (Hutton's)
Pompe Funebre
Prince Waterloo

Rex Mundi
Roi de Navarre
San Josef
Sir George Dackett
Surpasse Catafalque
Suwarrow
Semiramis
Vulcan
Walworth
Zeno

OF THE HYACINTH.

———

' Suave rubens Hyacinthus.'—VIRGIL.

———

IN the former edition of this book, I omitted all
notice of the Hyacinth, because, being very little
conversant with the culture of it, I did not consider
myself competent to give any directions respecting
it.   I now beg, to offer some practical observations
upon the treatment of this flower, which have been
communicated to me by a gentleman, who, having
occasion to visit Holland in the spring of 1821, spent
a few days at Haarlem, when the Hyacinths were in
flower, in a manner, as he reports, the most agreeable and gratifying.   He is a great admirer of the
flower-garden, and of an inquisitive turn of mind,
that prompts him to explore any subject thoroughly
to which he turns his attention.   I shall endeavour
to detail these observations in that conversational

mode as they took place between him and the Dutch
florists ; and as to the matter, it will speak for itself.
To me, at least, it appeared particularly interesting,
and if it fail of exciting interest here, it will be entirely owing to my inability to do justice to the report.

In the successful culture of this flower the Dutch
florists pride themselves more than in that of any
other, the Tulip not even excepted, and from the
immense yearly sale of which they derive a considerable profit, not only from this country, but I may
safely say from every state in Europe. No words
can express the self-complacency and satisfaction
which a Dutch florist feels in a fine sun-shining
morning in April, while exhibiting to some foreign
florist or traveller his spacious and richly-adorned
beds of this highly-perfumed flower, to him at once
a source of profit and of pleasure : his natural phlegm
and indifference seem to have vanished, and that
cold, reserved cast of national character to be laid
aside; pleasure sparkles in his eyes, increased, no
doubt, by the expectation of touching some fifty or
a hundred of your florins. The spectacle is truly

grand and magnificent; the order and arrangement admirable; and the fragrance powerful. Rows of red and yellow; purple and white of various shades follow in succession; and whole acres are covered with an immense mass of bloom.

'Can you produce anything equal to this in England?' demanded Mynheer Bloemist, with a smile of exultation; adding at the same time, 'you should study and adopt our method of cultivation.' My friend returned for answer, ' I fear your most approved mode of culture would not avail us much in England, without your soil and saline atmosphere, both of which seem so suitable and congenial to the growth of this flower.'

'Your observation is good,' replied Mynheer; ' but do not infer from thence that our care and culture are nothing, or that our pains to improve the soil is attended with no expense or trouble.'

'Your soil,' resumed my friend, ' has been described to me as belonging to that sort which is called alluvial—namely, a mixture of mud, sand, and other earths, which is generally left and depo-

sited in low lands after the subsiding of some vast
overflowing torrent or inundation, and that it bears
a great resemblance to that of Lower Egypt.'

' Our country,' replied Mynheer, ' is for the most
part naturally poor and barren. It may resemble
that of Egypt in some particulars, *viz.* its low situation and sandy earth ; but it is not yearly enriched
with the fertilizing slime, and mud and soil deposited
by the inundation of the Nile, which is said to be
caused by periodical rains that fall in Nubia and
Abyssinia ; there a hot sun in an unclouded atmosphere seems to impart birth and maturity to vegetable productions almost at the same instant; so
rapid is the growth, and so well matured the fruits
and grain ; there corn, and rice, and flax, sugar-
canes, vines, figs, and dates, melons, gourds, and
cucumbers, the papyrus, the lotus, &c. flourish in the
greatest luxuriancy. Take away our bulbs, and
what else have we to boast of? Choice exotics do
not thrive well with us, nor are our fruits too richly
flavoured ; we suffer more from damps and fogs than
you do in England.'

In the neighbourhood of Haarlem, in the province of South Holland, the greatest and principal display of hyacinths, tulips, jonquilles, irises, &c. is to be seen; and my friend visited in succession the gardens of George Voorhelm Schneevooght, of Henry Cornelis, of Theodore Storm, of H. Polman Mooy, and some others.

The Dutch florist has his tricks and finesse, as well as the English: he would persuade you, that when you have seen his collection, there is nothing in Holland besides worth looking at; his are the choicest, cheapest, and best; nor would he direct you, if he could possibly avoid it, to the residence or garden of any other florist. His tallies, or number-sticks, do not appear, and of course neither offend the eye nor take from the effect. If you ask him the name of a flower that has escaped his memory for the moment, he stoops down, scratches the ground with his fingers, feels for the concealed tally, and draws it up; which having examined, he replaces it again, and smooths the surface as it was before.

Petty robberies of flowers are not unfrequent among them, and at certain periods they are under the necessity of appointing watchmen to guard them. 'Pray, Mynheer Bloemist,' inquired my friend one day, 'what are the flowers you principally cultivate?' The answer he received was, 'the hyacinth, the tulip, the polyanthus-narcissus, the ranunculus, the anemone, the crocus, the jonquil, the bulbous iris, the gladiolus, the amaryllis, the rose, the lily, the dahlia, and a few other tuberous and bulbous-rooted plants, which seem by nature suited to our soil and climate, and in which our export trade in flowers principally consists. Of late years we have not paid much attention to the culture of the auricula, for in many parts of Holland the situation is too low and humid for this flower to continue in health long together. . Of all these our sale of hyacinths is by far the greatest: of late years we have sent a great many to the United States of America, and to Russia; but the demand for them from England is regular and constant: we have standing orders from the principal

K

seedsmen and florists in London and other parts of
England, as well as from Edinburgh and Dublin,
which we execute yearly; and this vast annual supply of hyacinths does not seem at all to affect the
demand in succeeding years.'

'Well, Mynheer Bloemist,' resumed my friend,
'I confess I feel exceedingly gratified with the sight
of your hyacinths; their perfume, beauty, and richness of colour, far surpass any idea that my mind
could have formed respecting them. At the proper
season, which you say is October, I wish you to
forward me to England one hundred roots of double
and one hundred of single, including all your finest
varieties of yellow, white, red, and blue. I particularly request to have the Bouquet Orange, Heroine,
Vainqueur, Favourite, and Pure d'Or included
among the yellow; Gloria Florum Suprema, Furius
Camillus, A-la-Mode, and Anna Maria Schuur-
mans among the white; Catherine, Victorieuse,
Waterloo, Comte de la Coste, Maria Louisa, among
the red; and Bouquet Constant, Gloria Mundi,
Helicon, l'Importante, and Pasquin among the
blue.'

'Your commands shall be executed with fidelity,' was the answer returned by Mynheer, accompanied with a bow expressive of the obligation and favour received.

'Now, Mynheer, when I receive those bulbs in England, I do not mean to be satisfied with one year's bloom, and then cast them away; I intend to try how far care and culture will assist me in preserving them, and in preventing that degeneracy, which our English gardeners say they so soon fall into; I shall therefore feel obliged to you for any information upon this subject which you may be disposed to impart, and upon which your experience so well enables you to speak.'

'You rate my poor abilities too highly, Sir,' answered Mynheer; 'and I fear you will be disappointed in the information which you seem desirous to obtain; for I have no particular methods to communicate, no successful experiments to detail, which are not known and practised by us all. Our soil round Haarlem is upon the whole poor and sterile, consisting of nearly two-thirds sand to one:

of loam, of a light brown colour, yet of considerable
depth; the nature of such a soil is of course light
and porous.   Observe with what facility I can force
my arm into this fresh-dug quarter, nearly to the
shoulder, yet by compression and treading we can
render it close and firm.   It is from the application
of animal dungs that you behold it here discoloured
and of a dark appearance.   Well rotten cow-dung
we find the best suited to such a soil, particularly in
that part of it in which we grow our hyacinths; yet
we never suffer it to come in contact with the bulbs.
When we apply it, we trench it in, a foot below
them; we refresh the soil above with leaf-mould
from time to time, and with occasional dressings of
maiden mould, where the ground has been exhausted
by long culture.   We have of late years applied
night-soil, dried and reduced to mould, with considerable advantage: I have no hesitation in saying,
that the brightness and vividness of the colours have
been greatly increased thereby.   There is one thing
in particular, which I wish you to observe with
minute attention: that is, not to cut the leaves off

the plants, after they have done flowering; but to suffer them to decay and die gradually, for the health, strength, and size of the bulb for the succeeding year depend upon its storing up a proper fund of sap, which you will in a great degree prevent by cutting off the leaves when in a green state. I recommend to you to cut down the flowering stem as soon as the bloom has faded, but by no means to deprive it of its leaves; great injury is done to all sorts of bulbs by this inconsiderate and unskilful practice. Great care is also requisite in drying the bulb, especially if May should be a rainy month; they will in that case require to be defended from the excessive rain. About the beginning of June, if the season has been dry and favourable, we begin to take them up; by that time the foliage has lost its sap, and become dry and decayed; we then cut it off within an inch of the bulb, but touch not the fibres. When this operation is finished, we replace them on the bed upon their sides, in rows according to the sorts, and cover them over about an inch deep with sand; this prevents the bulb from drying too fast and shrinking in substance. We suffer them to remain here a fortnight longer, till the fibres are dry and withered, and then consider them ripe, and fit to be taken up for good. After having carefully rubbed off the fibres, and any loose skins hanging to them, with a piece of soft woollen cloth, we take them into the house or store-rooms, where we arrange them in shallow boxes, one bulb deep, and cover them over with dry sand, where they remain till the planting season again comes round, which is the latter end of October; for if they were placed several together, they would be apt to heat, and liable to perish : such as are ordered and destined for exportation, we select at this time, and wrap up singly in paper.

' Were I to give any particular directions for forming the bed, I would recommend you, in the first place, to select such part of the garden as lies open and airy, with an exposure to the south or south-west, and which is protected by some building or fence on the north and east; the soil should be a good sandy loam, or, in absence thereof, fresh maiden earth, that has been dug six months at least before you use it; if twelve months, the better. To be enriched and incorporated with decayed leaf-mould, well rotten cow-dung, and river sand, in something like the following quantities :—

4 Barrows of maiden earth,
1 Do.   well rotten cow-dung,
2 Do.   leaf-mould,
2 Do.   sea or river sand.

' If you have the opportunity of adding to this one barrow of night-soil reduced to mould, no fitter or better compost can possibly be put together, and it will retain its strength and quality for two or three years : the trouble and expense, I admit, are considerable, but then you will be repaid by a fine bloom and healthy bulbs.

' If the subsoil be brick-earth or clay, which do not easily discharge the falling rains, the bed should be raised ten inches, at least, above the surface of the ground, that the bulbs may sustain no damage from them.   Plant them four inches deep, and nine inches apart every way, putting a little sand both

below and above the bulb, which not only prevents
the approach of insects, but acts as a drain around
it; but if the subsoil consist of sand or sandy gravel,
a stratum of four inches thick of rotten cow-dung
should be laid about a foot below the bulbs, which
will not only administer nourishment to the roots,
but preserve a cool bottom, in which they delight.
The bed should be hooped over, and mats thrown
on occasionally to keep off heavy and continued
rains, which sometimes fall in November, and are
followed by sharp frosts: these frosts are more liable
to injure the bulbs when the ground is saturated with
water than when it is moderately moist or dry; slight
frosts and gentle rains do no injury. Some florists
with small collections will cover the beds on the
approach of severe weather with old tan, to the
depth of six inches, which they remove in general, if
the weather permits, about the middle of February,
towards the end of which month, as well as in March,
when vegetation is in action, and the leaves begin to
shoot forth, a cold, bleak, easterly wind too frequently
prevails—a wind, as all travellers agree, congenial to

neither animal nor vegetable life in any part of the globe; in which case, a protection of upright hurdles, covered with mats, should be afforded, to arrest and turn aside the withering and chilling blast. Tulips require the same precaution. Except on these particular occasions, the bed should be exposed and open, and have a free circulation of air, without which no plants can thrive and continue healthy long together.

' About the commencement of April, in most seasons, these flowers begin to show colour; some are earlier than others, as is the case with most species of flowering plants; their stems then require to be tied loosely to sticks, to keep them upright,. and to support the weight of their bells; for if the weight does not break them, yet any sudden gust of wind would snap them in two, from their extremely brittle and succulent nature. It is necessary to protect the blossoms from the rays of the sun, if you wish to preserve their beauty and lustre; for three days' exposure, even to an April sun, would greatly impair their tints, and deaden the brilliancy of their

K 5

colours. Examine only the rich and glowing tint of
the damask-rose at five o'clock in the morning that
has opened in the night, and examine the same
again at ten, and you will be struck with the change
that five hours' sun has made. And it is no less
necessary to guard against any sudden return of
frost at this season, which not unfrequently occurs;
the covering of stout canvas ought to be let down close
to the ground, and mats thrown over beside; for the
injury done to the bloom by frost is more sudden and
serious than that done by the sun. By attending to
these two necessary precautions, I have no doubt but
that you will be enabled to preserve the bloom in
high order and beauty for three weeks or more.

‘ These, Sir, are my directions for the culture of
the Hyacinth; any further minute detail I conceive
unnecessary, as your own good sense and judgment
will supply the deficiency. I am not aware that I
have omitted anything essential. As to the plan we
pursue in raising new varieties from seed, you have
already inferred that you have no wish for me to
enter upon that subject, but that you will be content

to leave the raising of seedlings in the hands of the Dutch florist, with all its care, trouble, and advantages.'

' Allow me, Mynheer,' rejoined my friend, ' to return you my hearty thanks for this excellent botanical lecture, if I may so term it, to which I have listened with peculiar satisfaction; if I fail in the successful culture of my bulbs, with these clear methodical directions before me, I shall most certainly attribute it to my unskilful application of them.'

With a hearty shake of the hand my friend and Mynheer Bloemist then separated, perfectly satisfied with each other.

This flower is certainly not so extensively cultivated among us as many others that are less beautiful and inviting; this arises, I am inclined to think, from the vulgar notion—which, by the bye, may be, after all, a vulgar error—that the bulbs are hardly worth cultivating a second year in Britain, and are, therefore, like the Guernsey Lily, cast away as useless.

I have not the least doubt but that in many parts

of England, were the experiment fairly made, the hyacinth might be cultivated with success; the spot chosen ought to be situated near to the sea-coast, and the soil a light sandy earth of tolerable depth. I am told this flower thrives well in Devonshire; and there are many florists, within the circle of my acquaintance, who yearly bloom from a hundred to two hundred bulbs; and, according to the account given by them, with tolerable success in general, both as regards the fineness of the blossom and the condition of the bulb when taken up. There is a rich tract of land by the side of the Humber, and along the banks of the Trent in Yorkshire, where the finest kidney potatoes in all England are raised, with clear skins, free from all speck and scab; bulbs of all sorts, I am satisfied, would thrive in this soil, and that they would rise with clear skins and silvery coats, equal to those imported from Holland.

I hold it the extreme of folly in any one, who has a garden, to cast away the roots which have flowered in glasses, much less those in pots; the thousands that are suffered to perish in this way every year in

London is astonishing: one year's accumulation of
these cast-away bulbs would produce an ample stock
for an experimental florist to commence an essay
with. If by chance a few bulbs perish in the bed
during winter, care must be taken to make a reserve
against such loss, by planting a dozen bulbs or so in
pots to supply their places, by plunging the pots in
the ground, and thereby keep up the order and uni-
formity of the bed; such as are not wanted may be
taken into the house, and forced into flower early.
The usual mode which the London florists pursue in
keeping these bulbs in pots through the winter, is to
plunge them in sand or coal-ashes up to the rim, and
to cover them with six inches of old tan : in February they begin to remove some from this repository
into the green-house to force; and so continue to do,
from time to time, as they want them. I know of no
better method.

The following flowers, with the prices, are copied
from a Dutch Catalogue : the gulden or guilder or
Dutch florin are of the same value, 1s. 9d. English;
a stiver $1\frac{1}{20}d$. English.

DOUBLE HYACINTHS.

YELLOW.

	Guild.	Stiv.
Bouquet Orange	2	0
Chrysolora	0	6
Duc de Berry	0	10
Heroine	15	0
L'Or Végétable	0	6
Louis d'Or	0	12
Ophir	0	6
Pure d'Or	3	0
Vainqueur	2	0

WHITE.

	Guild.	Stiv.
Aardshertogin	0	12
Admiral Zoutman	0	4
A-la-Mode	0	10
Altesse Royale	0	6
A. M. Schuurmans	1	0
Blanche Fleur	0	4
Bailluw Van Zuidwyk	0	4
Baron Van Wassenaar	0	6
Beauté sans Pareille	0	10
———— Tendre	0	10
Belle Forme	0	4

	Guild.	Stiv.
Bijou des Amateurs	0	6
Cœur Tendre	0	4
Cœur Aimable	0	4
Constantia Elizabeth	0	4
Couronne Blanche	0	3
Dageraad	0	3
Diana Van Ephese	0	10
Duc de Berry	0	6
Don Gratuit	0	6
Duc de Penthievre	0	6
Furius Camillus	1	10
Gloria Florum	1	6
Grande Blanche Imperiale	0	15
Grand Monarque	0	12
Gilde Vryheid	0	4
Hermione	0	4
Illustre Beauté	0	6
Juno	0	10
Madame de St. Simon	0	10
Minerva	0	6
Nannette	0	6
Sphæra mundi	0	12
Réviseur Général	0	6
Sultan Achmet	0	8
Staten Général	0	10
Violet Superbe	0	4
Virgo	0	6

RED.

	Guild.	Stiv.
Augustus Rex	0	5
Boerhaven	0	6
Bruidskleed	0	6
Catherine Victorieuse.	3	0
Comte de la Coste	3	0
Couronne d'Or	1	0
Délice du Printems	0	8
Diadème de Flore	0	6
Duchesse de Parme	0	8
Eleonora	0	6
Emilia Galotti	0	8
Flos Sanguineus.	0	8
Grootvorst	0	8
Hugo Grotius	0	6
Illustre Pyramidale	0	0
Il Pastor Fido	0	4
La Délicatesse	0	8
La Superbe Royale	0	4
L'honneur d'Amsterdam	0	10
Maria Louisa.	1	10
Madame Zoutman	0	12
Marquise de la Coste	1	0
Perruque Quarré	0	8
Phœnix	0	4
Rex Rubrorum	0	8
Rose agréable	0	5
Rose d'Ispahan	0	12

	Guild.	Stiv.
Rose Illustre	0	0
—— Mignon.	0	6
—— Sceptre	1	0
Rouge Charmant.	0	6
Rozenkrans Van Flora.	0	6
Roxane.	0	12
Sans Rival	0	8
Soleil Royal	0	10
Superbissima	0	10
Temple van Apollo	0	6
Waterloo	1	6

———

BLUE.

A-la-Mode	0	6
Alcibiades	0	6
Bouquet Constant	3	0
Bucentaurus.	0	6
Bleu Foncé.	0	6
Cœruleus Imperialis.	0	4
Drusus	0	8
Directeur Général	0	8
Duc de Luxembourg	0	8
—— de Normandie.	0	8
—— de Bronswic	0	6
Flora Perfecta	0	6
Globe Celeste.	0	12

	Guild.	Stiv.
—— Terrestre	0	6
Graaf Floris	0	8
Grandeur Triomphante	0	12
Grand Gris-de-Lin	0	10
Gloria Mundi	3	0
Helicon	3	0
Incomparable Azur	0	4
Keizer Tiberius	0	4
Kroon van Indien	0	8
La Bien Aimée	0	4
La Gentilesse	1	0
L'Amitie	0	4
L'Illustre	0	8
L'Importante	4	0
La Ville de Haarlem	0	8
Mirabeau	0	12
Mon Bijou	0	8
—— Ami	0	6
Negro Superbe	0	12
Nigritienne	0	6
Olden Barneveld	0	5
Parmenio	0	8
Passe ne plus ultra	1	0
Pasquin	0	12
Porceleine Sceptre	0	6
Velours Pourpre	0	3

SINGLE HYACINTHS.

THE names of a few of the finest, the prices of which run nearly the same as for the double.

YELLOW.

Couleur de Jonquille	Prince d'Orange
Pluie d'Or	Toison d'Or

WHITE.

Armenia	Melpoméné
Belle Amazone	Premier noble Thais
Hercules	

RED.

Actrice	L'Eclatante
Aimable Rosette	Mignon
Aimable Louise	Princesse d'Esterhazy
Fleur des Dâmes	Regina Rubrorum Thalia
L'Eclair	Vuurlam

BLUE.

Alexander Niger	Konings
Buonaparte	Grande Védette
Dolphin	La Modeste
Fortunatus	Nonpareille
Colbert	Orondates
General Hoche	Staten Général

OF THE ROSE.

'*Rosa mea.*'—PLAUTUS.

'Rose thou art the sweetest flower
That ever drank the amber shower.'
T. MOORE.

'I know a bank whereon the wild Thyme blows,
Where Oxlip and the nodding Violet grows,
O'er-canopied with luscious Woodbine,
With sweet Musk Roses, and with Eglantine:
There sleeps Titania.'
SHAKSPEARE'S *Midsummer Night's Dream.*

To say anything in praise of the attractive beauty
and sweetness of the Rose, would be not only to insult the good sense and good taste of my readers, but
absolutely to imply the want of both; suffice it then
to say, that the Rose is a universal favourite; and
that in no part of the world, torrid, temperate, or
frigid, but ' nascuntur rosæ,' of some description or
other. Among the ancients the Rose was consecrated to Venus—' flos Veneri sacer'—and was considered by them the harbinger of spring.

TUSCAN ROSE.

Pub.ly Whittaker Treacher &C.° Ave Maria Lane

A Ducôte. Lithog.her Maria Lane

' Cum rosam viderit, tunc iucipere ver arbitratur.'

CICERO.

The Roman guests at feasts and entertainments adorned their heads with it, as ' convivæ rosis coronabantur;' thus Horace:

' Mitte sectari, rosa quo locorum
      sera moretur.'

Again:

' Huc vina, et unguenta, et nimium breves
Flores amænæ ferre jube rosæ.'

And again in another place:

' Cur nou sub altâ vel platano, vel hâc
Pinu jacentes sic temere, et rosâ
      Canos odorati capillos
Dum licet, Assyriâque nardo
Potamus uncti? Dissipat Evius
Curas edaces.'

Persons when probably ill and anxious to live, used to express themselves thus, ' I hope I shall live to gather roses another year:'

' Alias tractare rosas.'—JUVENAL.

Ovid makes mention of ' amæna rosaria;' and Virgil, while living in retirement at Parthenope, in the south of Italy, which was soon after pulled down, and rebuilt under the name of Neapolis, or new city, now called Naples:

' Illo Virgilium me tempore dulcis alebat
  Parthenope, studiis florentem ignobilis oti ;'

intimated an intention which he then entertained of
writing upon horticulture, and the rose in particular,
as cultivated in gardens at Pæstum in Lucania,
which he mentions thus towards the end of the fourth
Georgic :

' Forsan et pingues hortos quæ cura colendi
  Ornaret, canerem, biferique rosaria Pæsti.'

Ausonius, likewise a perfect amateur of the rose,
and who wrote upon it, an author, by-the-bye, that
I have not been able to lay my hand on, says,

' Vidi pæstano gaudere rosaria cultu.'

The roses principally noticed by Latin authors
are, the rosa Damascena, or white rose of Damascus;
rosa Milesia, or red rose of two varieties, rubra et
purpurea; rosa provincialis, called also Batavia, or
the large Provence, which was first discovered in the
neighbourhood of Toulouse; rosa pæstana, or bas-
tard musk, which flowered twice in the year, in May
and again in September; rosa moschata vel odorata,
the African and Asiatic musk rose; rosa holoserica,
or velvet rose : there were also the hyberna, or early

flowering; the scrotina, or late flowering; and the Grecian luteola, or yellow.

The varieties of the rose are now extremely numerous; many are the native or natural productions of foreign countries, and many are the productions of European florists from seed.

The Scotch roses, that have been raised from seed within these few years past, are exceedingly fine and delicate, and make a great addition to the flower-garden.

I might have remarked before, that the rose-gardens of Pæstum were as celebrated in the time of Augustus, in honour of whom the month of August was named, as those of Mr. Lee of Hammersmith, or Mr. Loddige of Hackney, in our time. In his reign literature was encouraged, and the liberal arts and sciences began to flourish; and this love of letters and of the arts was soon followed by a refinement of taste and manners, that shortly after brought into use all the expensive embellishments, as well as the more elegant conveniences of life: the simple farm-house and the plain cabbage-garden of their

ancestors were changed into splendid villas and magnificent gardens, adorned with fountains, statues,
and flowering shrubs and plants.   An indecent statue
of Priapus was stuck up in all gardens, as ' Hortûs
custos.'

My object in introducing this flower into my treatise, is for the more immediate purpose, than any
other I had in view, of presenting a select catalogue
of the finest sorts, distinguished alike for varied tints,
fragrance, and beauty, and which will, in fact, form
a most complete and magnificent rosary, well deserving of cultivation.

Rose-trees grow best in a light rich loam, and
require to be well pruned every year, to enable them
to throw out strong flowering buds: these buds are
very often destroyed in the spring by a small, dark
red grub, which feeds upon them, folds itself up in
the leaves, and then changes into a moth chrysalis.
In the seasons they prevail, if not sought for and
destroyed, there will be but few early Roses, the
only chance remaining will be in the formation of
fresh summer buds.   They are also liable to be

injured by a small, light green caterpillar, which is also found to infest the apple blossom and the young forming fruit, and which feeds upon it. When the trees are blighted with honey-dew, or infested with the green fly, they ought to be washed with strong soap-suds, or cleansed with a soft brush dipped in a lye of lime-water, sulphur, and tobacco.

Propagation is by dividing the roots, by budding on the briar, and by layers laid down the beginning of July. As a skilful gardener is not always at hand to perform this last-named method of propagation, I will endeavour briefly to describe it, and which some of my readers, perhaps, may be inclined to perform themselves.

Select the strong young shoots that have been formed the same year; then, with a sharp budding or other thin-bladed knife, begin a quarter of an inch below the joint, and make an incision of three-quarters of an inch in length on the side next the ground, up the middle of the shoot; after which, cut off transversely the nib or extremity of the tongue just below the joint; then move the ground, and

L

open a place three inches deep, in which, after having first put a little sand, or sand and fresh loam
mixed, fix and peg down the layer to that depth,
and after giving the tongue a little twist or turn on
one side, to keep the cleft open, close the earth tight
round it. When the whole is performed, give the
layers a gentle watering to settle the mould, and
which ought to be repeated from time to time, to
promote the striking of the new fibres, and to keep
the mother-plant in a healthy, growing state. The
layers, in most cases, will be fit to remove the spring
following; but such as are not well rooted had better
remain till the succeeding autumn. The same mode
of operation may be applied to most shrubs; and
take care to cover that part of the shoot only with
earth which is pegged down,—the other part of it,
connected with the stool or parent plant, must lie
uncovered.

Catalogue of Roses.

WHITE.

White Monthly	White Damask
Double White	Double Musk
White Provence	Rosa Banksia
Rose Blanche de Belgique	

MOSS.

Red Moss	Scarlet Moss
White Moss	Blush Moss
Single Moss	Mossy Rose de Meaux

SCOTCH.

Double White Scotch	Double Marble Scotch
——— Red Scotch	——— Purple Scotch
——— Blush Scotch	——— Pale Yellow Scotch
——— Scotch Provence	Fairy Scotch Rose

BLUSH.

Great Maiden's Blush	Shailer's Provence
Lesser Maiden's Blush	Dutch Provence
Celestial	Imperial Blush
Blush Provence	Blush Mignon
——— Belgique	Brunswick
Early Blush	Aurora

L 2

SWEET BRIARS.

Semi Double Sweet Briar	Royal Sweet Briar
Double Sweet Briar	Monstrous Sweet Briar
Manning's Blush Sweet Briar	Mossy Sweet Briar
	Double Tree Sweet Briar

RED.

Swiss Rose	Rose of Four Seasons
Common Provence	Red Mignon
Tree Pæony Rose	Superb Red
Spongs	Royal Red
Italian	Rose de Meaux
Dutch Tree	Rosa Bullata
Red Monthly	

BRIGHT RED.

Carmine	Bright Crumpled
Proliferous Carmine	Neapolitan
Fiery	Mogul
Refulgent	Cluster
Scarlet Provence	Superb Carmine
Rosa Pæstana	

DARK.

Tuscan	Pluto
Triumphant	Burning Coal

Mourning	Black Frizzled
Large Dark China	—— Mottled
Castile	Double Velvet
Negro	Mexican

PURPLE.

Bright Purple	Light Purple
Royal Purple	Grand Purple
Red and Violet	Blue
Favourite Purple	—— and Purple
Blue Purple	Mottled Purple

YELLOW.

Single Yellow	Double Yellow

RED AND WHITE.

York and Lancaster	Striped Mignon
Rosa Mundi	

OF GERANIUMS.

THE following select catalogue of geraniums * comprehends some of the newest, rarest, and most admired varieties :—

Dianthiflorum
Eximium
Baileyanum
Macranthon
Tricolour
Floridum
Pavonium
Daveyanum
Rubescens
Involucratum
Ardens
Nervosum
Hoareanum
Bicolour
Flammidum
Obscurum
Ignescens, Majus

Coriaceum
Sanguineum
Villosum
Dawsonianum
Thompsonianum
Reticulatum
Oblatum
Triumphans
Cordifolium Novum
Foliaceum, Majus
Pes Pelicanum
Crassicaule
Formosum
Fulgidum
Lumleyanum
Mooreanum

* Geraniums grow luxuriantly in my carnation compost.

OF THE GEORGINA.

Tнιs flower was introduced about the year 1804, by Lady Holland, from Spain. It is a native of Mexico, in South America, the part from whence potatoes were first brought to England by Sir Walter Raleigh, in the year 1565. The roots are susceptible of frost, and liable to be destroyed by it; of course they must be taken up every year, and kept in dry sand, with the crown uppermost. It is propagated by dividing the roots; a single tuber even will suffice, by cuttings and by seed. In many instances it will sow itself, for plants very frequently spring up on the spot where it has stood the preceding year. It is now generally treated as an annual, by sowing the seed in March, upon heat; the young plants are pricked out singly into small pots, and kept in frames until May, when they may be turned into the ground to flower in the

autumn. To ensure an early bloom in the summer,
the old roots are planted in pots in March, and kept
in the green-house till all danger of the frost is past.
This flower, from its great height and size, is too
large for a small flower-garden: half a dozen roots
are enough for a large one. It is best adapted to
fill up the vacancies in ornamental shrubberies,
where it makes a grand and magnificent appearance,
through the summer and autumn. The double
flowers are now most cultivated, for the finest
varieties of which we are indebted to the French;
their colours are white, crimson, scarlet, yellow, and
purple of different shades.

OF THE

RUSSIAN AND DANISH STOCKS.

OF all the flowers that have of late years been introduced into England, none seem to give greater pleasure than the different varieties of these annual or ten week stocks; and none are sought after at this moment with greater avidity : they consist of about eighteen sorts, and form a splendid flower-garden of themselves. The colours which I have noticed, and which are thus described upon some packets of the seed sent from Denmark: light red, tile red, dark red or mahogany, ruby, scarlet, flesh-colour, peach blossom, light ash, dark ash, lilac, blue, purple, mulberry, black, white, &c. Some of the plants have the wall-flower leaf, and others the Brompton leaf. Before the introduction of these, we were acquainted only with the scarlet, the purple, and the white. The seed ought to be sown about the middle of September, and the young plants to be pricked out three or four in small pots, and to be protected in frames through the winter; these will flower early in the spring. The seed may be sown again in March or April, for plants to bloom in the summer. Some biennial or winter stocks have also been introduced, but I have yet had no opportunity of seeing them flower. In mentioning these, I have no wish to underrate our native stock, the Brompton, which in some situations grows to an immense size, presenting one large mass of bloom : the brilliant colour of the scarlet is the most striking, but the purple and the white are equally pleasing. The seed of the Brompton ought to be sown some time in May, that the stalks may get hard and woody to stand the winter; the careful gardener, when in possession of a good double-flowering scarlet, will not neglect to winter some of the plants in pots, either in frames, green-houses, or under hoops covered with mats, during any very hard frosts; for good and well-saved seed of this stock is not always to be got.

If I may credit the testimony of a gardener of

the name of Davis, who works for me occasionally, and I have no reason to doubt his testimony, he assures me, that about thirty years ago, during the time of his apprenticeship to Mr. Mott, gardener to the Duke of Bolton, at Hackwood, in Hampshire, his Grace received from Germany, through the medium of a domestic servant, whose father was a gardener in that country, the same coloured stocks as I have been describing; they were considered a great rarity, and were much admired, but they were called Grecian stocks, the name they now go by in France. The major part of them, he says, were wall-leafed.

The annual stock is, I believe, originally a native of Greece, and called 'cheiranthus,' or hand-flower, probably from its being carried in the hand as a nosegay, or making a handful of flowers. There is no doubt, in my opinion, but that these stocks found their way from Greece into Russia, Denmark, and the north of Europe, and since our unrestricted intercourse with the Continent, the seed of them has reached England, bringing with it the name of the

country from which it was imported.   It is not, however, worth my while to cavil either about the name
or origin, for I give them a free welcome to the garden; and as for their recommendation and passport,
they carry them with them.

———

HERBACEOUS PLANTS.

THE finely flowering plants of this description decorate the garden in an eminent degree; they flower year after year, and require little or no care. Many kinds contain distinct species, and these species again consist of numerous and beautiful varieties. The following list is select, yet comprehensive.

Aconitum	Convolvulus
Achillea	Coreopsis
Allium	Delphinium
Alyssum	Fraxinella
Anthericum	Fumaria
Arabis	Gentiana
Asclepias	Gladiolus
Asphodelus	Hepatica
Caltha	Hemerocallis
Campanula	Hieracium
Catananche	Iris
Centaurea	Liatris
Chelone	Linum
Chrysocoma	Lychnis

Lythrum

Melittis

Monarda

Narcissus

Œnothera

Orchis

Ornithogalum

Orobus

Phlox

Polygala

Rudbeckia

Saponaria

Saxifraga

Scilla

Silene

Statice

Teucrium

Trollius

Veratrum

Verbascum

Veronica

I have given the generic names of the above, because they are more generally known and expressed by them; I shall add the English names of a few more, as they occur to my recollection.

Candy Tuft

Columbine

Daisy

Dogs'-tooth Violet

Lily

Poppy

Rose Campion

Rock Rose

Wall Flower

Sweet William

Heart's Ease

Honesty

Jonquil

Peony

Foxglove

Solomon's Seal

Lily of the Valley

Rocket

Hollyhock

Valerian

Loose strife

Scabious

TENDER AND HARDY ANNUALS.

Balsam	Lavatera
Cockscomb	Lupine
Eggplant	Sweet Pea
Tricolor	Belvidere
Globe Amaranth	Persicaria
India Pink	Hawkweed
Xeranthemum	Sweet Sultan
Zinnia	French Marigold
Larkspur	African ditto
Chrysanthemum	

OF

ORNAMENTAL TREES

AND

FLOWERING SHRUBS.

I KNOW of no scene in nature more interesting than a well-planted Shrubbery, stored with choice trees, where art imitates nature, and where a judicious classification and grouping have been observed, both as regards the height, the form, and colour; so that all the various shades of leaf, of branch, and blossom, blend and harmonize in order and beauty.

In the spring of the year in particular, such a scene never fails to interest even the most heartless and indifferent beholder; he finds his senses refreshed and gladdened by the gentle breeze, wafting the sweets from so many flowers, varied alike in form and fragrance: nay, his whole frame feels most sensibly at the time, that there is a 'healing' in the

air around him, and he inhales it with delight. Nor
is the appearance of the Shrubbery in autumn much
less striking; the pendant berries and the changeful
leaf, exhibiting such diversity of shade and colour,
give to it a most picturesque effect, lovely, though
somewhat mournful.

When one reflects indeed upon the length of time,
the toil, the trouble, and the vast expense, that have
necessarily been incurred in transplanting into England from so many different countries, and bringing
as it were into one view, these elegant and useful
productions of nature, one cannot but be struck with
the patient and persevering industry of man, and
the force and application of his intellectual faculties
even in this pursuit; of which these exotic shrubs
and trees may be considered as lasting monuments,
growing in honour of all those, who have been so
fortunate as to have benefited their country by the
contribution of some new species or variety.

The courteous reader may here, if he feel so inclined, not having the splendid reality before him,
indulge awhile in 'wakeful reverie,' and fancy

himself in the centre of some spacious grove-belted lawn, contemplating such a scene; and if he further fancy himself in the company of a beloved wife, daughter, friend, or companion, all the better; for to be alone in such a case, is beyond doubt, lonely;— the Rose and the Violet, plucked and presented by the hand of any one of these, will at the time be prized the more; and the elegant and lovely Lilac, Jasmine, Honeysuckle, Sweet Briar, and the Virgin's Bower, will appear to shed fresh sweets unnoticed before; and as two pair of eyes, according to every-day cal- culation, will discover more beauties than one, so two minds, if the least congenial in taste, will, from the pleasing interchange of observation and sentiment, and a disposition to please and be pleased, expe- rience, double gratification in examining the lovely and interesting objects before them.

Let the reader, as I repeated before, contemplate such a scene of Nature, where trees and shrubs (on whose branches the birds are warbling their sweet notes) rise gradually above one another, in form not much unlike to the interior seats and stages

of some vast amphitheatre; the front occupied with
plants of short growth, yet of the choicest flowering
sorts, and the back ground filled up with ornamental
trees of taller size: let him there view in succession
the early blossoms in January, February, and March
of the

Mezereon	Spurge Laurel
Pyracantha	Almond
Laurustinus	Phillyrea
Glastonbury Thorn	Peach Tree
Alaternus	Portugal Laurel
Manna Ash	Spanish Traveller's Joy
Cornelian Cherry	

And again in April, May, June, and July, the

Bay Tree	Guelder Rose
Barberry Tree	Jasmine
Corchorus, from Japan	Judas Tree
Honeysuckle	Kalmia
Hypericum	Rose
Laurel	Syringo
Laburnum	Sweet Briar .
Lilac	Cistus
Privet	Service Tree
Elder	Hawthorn
Furze	Horse Chestnut

Magnolia	Sumach
Scarlet Maple	Althæa
Rhododendron	Broom
Mountain Ash	Heath
Bird Cherry	Pomegranate
Rose Acacia	Passion Flower
Tulip Tree	Spiræa
Azalea	Tamarisk
Bladder Senna	Trumpet Flower
Itea	Virgin's Bower, &c.

Nor let him overlook these evergreens, the

Andromeda	Cypress
Box	Arbutus
Coronilla	Bignonia
Germander	Rockrose
Arbor Vitæ	Juniper
Cedar	Southern Wood
Fir	Ivy
Holly	Savin
Cytisus	Widow's Wail

There are many other trees of tall growth, which more properly belong to the park, the wood, and the forest, as

Ash	Chesntut
Alder	Cork Tree
Beech	Elm
Birch	Lime

Larch	Sycamore
Oak	Walnut
Plane	Willow, &c.
Poplar	

. In gardens the choicest flowering shrubs of dwarfish growth only should be introduced ; for few plants thrive well beneath the smothering shade of large ones : and in forming new shrubberies and plantations, especial care should be taken to allow proper space for the several plants, lest in a few years they become a tangled wood, and require untimely lopping, which not only injures their growth but destroys their beauty.

THE BOWER.

‘ The roof
Of thickest covert was inwoven shade.
Laurel and Myrtle, and what higher grew
Of firm and fragrant leaf; on either side
Acanthus, and each odorous bushy shrub
Fenced up the verdant wall ; each beauteous flower,
Iris all hues, Roses and Jessamin,
Rear’d high their flourish’d heads between, and wrought
Mosaic ; under foot the Violet,
Crocus, and Hyacinth, with rich inlay,
Broider’d the ground.’

MILTON.

How grand, stately, and majestic appear those large
Elms, Beech trees, Oaks, Planes, and Sycamores,
which are pretty generally to be met with in most of
our noblemen's parks in England; whose branches
have never been violated by the axe, but have been
suffered to grow by way of ornament, descending on
all sides within eight or ten feet of the ground, and
thereby affording a most agreeable shade and shelter
to both men and cattle ! I have always viewed them
with pleasure.

I here recommend to my youthful readers to seize
every opportunity of acquiring not only a knowledge
of the names, but also of the several properties of each
tree and shrub; and to be able readily to distinguish
the same both by leaf, flower, and fruit. They will
find their perception quickened, and their compre-
hension enlarged, by a close examination into the
various productions of nature; and their gratification
will increase, as their knowledge of natural history
advances; for it is really provoking oftentimes to
witness the ignorance of many persons, (not Cock-
neys alone,) on the subject of trees and plants in
particular, who are well informed upon almost every
other.

A

FLOWER CHRISTENING.

One of the most important and wished-for events in the life of a florist—in a florist's estimation, at least —is the raising of a fine flower from seed. His joy on first beholding it is equal to that of a lord on first viewing the infant heir of his title, wealth, and honours. By the production of this flower he claims the undisputed title of florist among the brotherhood, grounds his pretensions to superior knowledge, and assumes a loftier tone of decision upon every disputable point connected with the fancy. But to fix upon an appropriate and distinguished name for his new flower, is a work of almost as much difficulty as to raise it. No vulgar or common name can, in his opinion, speak its merits or exemplify its beauties. The flower must be ennobled by the ennobling name of King, Queen, Emperor, Hero, and very often consecrated by the sacred titles of Jupiter, Mars, Juno, Venus. The unlettered florist, on such an occasion, is frequently obliged to consult the parson, the schoolmaster, or the doctor, as high authorities, for some learned and astounding name; but the summary of the proper names of the heathen gods and goddesses, illustrious heroes and heroines, and celebrated worthies and beauties of antiquity, discovered at the end of Entick's Spelling Dictionary, has obviated much of the difficulty heretofore complained of. Sam Greenhorn, an old florist, after many years trying and toiling, at length had the good luck to raise a number of seedling Carnations, which dazzled the eyes, excited the envy, and blinded the judgment, not only of Sam, but of many others in his neighbourhood. Sam, with nice discrimination, selected twelve of the best, and hastened up with ardent speed to town, a distance of fifty miles, to present them for exhibition at a flower-show society, whose members were met to contend for a silver cup, and celebrate their annual feast; it was somewhere near Chelsea

M

or Battersea, places noted for the cutting of simples
and cabbages, as well as the curing of simpletons.

Sam's name was announced by the landlord in
due form, and he was ordered to be ushered up stairs.
He entered the room, made his reverence to the
chairman, and presented his seedlings. They were
most minutely inspected and critically examined;
and whether it was the smile of pleasure and approbation that appeared on their countenances, accompanied with sly winks, becks, and leers, or that
roguish, malicious, mischievous smile, which is often
visible when simple men become the dupes of their
own weakness and credulity, and the sport of others,
I am at a loss to determine: all declared themselves
struck with astonishment, and professed an eager
desire to become subscribers and purchasers of these
new flowers; no language, according to their account,
could sufficiently describe their beauties, and no price
could overrate their value. Sam was left to fix his
own price, and fancied his purse to be already filled,
like the cornucopia of old, and his reputation as a

florist established for ever. A difficulty was started because those seedlings had not yet been named, and therefore had no distinguishing titles whereby to know them. Sam was requested to retire for a while for this purpose, and particularly charged to fix handsome names to them. He withdrew accordingly, not a little perplexed at the task he had to perform. It is true, he had been pondering in his mind for months over the names he should give them, but had not been able to come to any final conclusion. He could have no benefit of clergy in this case, because he was a bit of a methodist; as to the schoolmaster, he said it was of no use to go to him, for he only taught upon the national system, and therefore did not know more than himself; and as to the doctor in his neighbourhood, there was a little bill unpaid on his wife's account, which foreclosed the door of application in that quarter. ' When I get to London,' Sam used to say, ' I shall get over this dilemma about names;' for London, he had heard, was the place where honours, titles, and distinctions, were conferred; and that if they were once christened there, nobody would presume hereafter to change them.

On descending below, he found ten or twelve persons seated round a large table, drinking porter, smoking tobacco, and betting upon the pans of flowers of their respective masters; for our London tip-top florists never go unattended to those feasts. Sam was invited to drink, and a few moments' conversation soon put them all upon one convivial footing of good fellowship. He began to find himself quite at home, and thought himself extremely lucky in the opportunity thus afforded him of asking their advice and counsel; in truth, these fellows generally know as much or more about flowers than their employers, for they are the operative florists, while the others, in general, are only lookers-on. Sam took from the box his best scarlet-bizarred Carnation, and desired the company to give a name to it.

Tom Tulip, as the oldest fancier in the room, took the lead upon the occasion, and swore that it was all over a good flower, and nothing but a good one, and that if ever flower deserved the name of

Emperor, this one did, and he therefore proposed
that it should be called Greenhorn's Emperor, which
was unanimously agreed to.   The bell was rung,
the waiter came, and two bottles of wine were
ordered by Sam, upon the suggestion of Tulip.
Chair! chair! was called, and Mr. Samuel Greenhorn was unanimously voted into it.   The wine
arrived, the corks were drawn in a crack, and Tom
Tulip proposed the health of Mr. Greenhorn with
three, and success to his Emperor.   The bottles
were soon emptied in discussing the imperial properties of the Emperor.   Sam then drew forth a
purple-flaked carnation, which was handed round.
Bill Rose descanted for some time upon the various
merits of this flower, pointed out the real Tyrian
purple stripe, and maintained that it was one of the
best he ever had seen : the name, he insisted, should
be Greenhorn's Queen,—Queen Caroline.   Sam
nodded ascent, and ordered in a third bottle, which
was soon disposed of as before.   A rose-coloured
flake was next handed round.   Strawberry Jack
declared himself enraptured with it; the leaf was a

complete rose leaf, well ribboned, well formed, and
the colour that of the royal Provence rose, bright
and brilliant. Jack swore that Mr. Greenhorn was
one of the luckiest fellows he ever knew in his life,
and that the flower should be called the Rose of
Roses ; this name was also adopted. A fresh bottle
was called for, and the baptismal toast drunk as
before with glee. The spirits of the company began
now to be volatilized, and the tones of their voices
mellowed and heightened ; they were all talkers
and no hearers ; a charming discord of merry sounds
or songs was also heard, and coarse jokes cracked as
thick as nuts. The exhaustion of the bottle produced a pause, and another flower was brought forward, a crimson bizarre. Ned Ricklas undertook
to point out its beauties. ' Observe here,' cries
Ned, ' the genuine colours of the rainbow ; here's
crimson, scarlet, and purple, softened down in a
variety of shades : I mean to call this, for I am
a bit of a botanist,' said Ned, ' after old father
Linnæus, a flower worthy of him, and he of the
flower.' A peal of approbation followed : Green-

horn ordered another bottle, Linnæus's health was
drank in raptures, and the same etiquette was observed as before. A scarlet flake was next produced, and Greenhorn declared that he would name
it himself. Moonlight Dick held the flower in his
hand. ' Well, Mr. Greenhorn,' he exclaimed, ' this
is a wonder of a flower; this is a flamer; I can look
the sun in the face easier than this flower, its bright
scarlet quite overcomes me; what pretty name have
you for it?' ' Why, as to the matter of that,' said
Sam, ' I don't know much about prettiness, but I
mean to call it after my wife, Meg.' ' Why now,'
replied Dick, ' that's both handsomely said and
kindly done of you; it shall be named the Lovely
Margaret by all means, and we will toast her in a
bumper.'

The sixth bottle was called for, which the landlord, being now at leisure, after having attended
upon the company up stairs, brought in himself,
and inquired, in rather a sharpish tone, who was to
pay for all this wine, beer, tobacco, and sundries?
He held the bill, at the same time, in his hand,

amounting to somewhere about seven and forty shillings, including Greenhorn's refreshment, before he waited upon the company up stairs. ‘ Oh,’ exclaims Tom Tulip, ‘ our chairman there, Mr. Samuel Greenhorn, will stand godfather to his own seedlings, and discharge the bill with pleasure; but we have not yet got half through the ceremony: it will never do to send the rest home into the country without their names; what say you, Mr. Greenhorn ?’

‘ I will just step out and settle with mine host for what we have had in,’ replied Sam, ‘ and I will return presently.’ Sam, it is true, felt elevated with liquor; but this unthought-of call upon his slender and ill-provided purse, which happened luckily to contain, within two or three shillings, the sum demanded, brought him to sober recollection. The landlord took what he had, and Sam, it being then near ten o'clock, decamped in silence, leaving his Emperor, Queen, Rose of Roses, old Linnæus, and his wife Meg, behind him. The deep, arch rogues, his companions, these modern Cantelupes, hearing that Greenhorn had decamped, rushed vexed and disappointed into the street, and sent forth shouts of scorn, insult, and derision; these appalling sounds were yet within reach of Sam's ears, and quickened with alarm his reeling steps. His Emperor, they bawled out, was a mere button; his Queen a butter-cup; Linnæus no better than a wind-mill sail; his Tyrian purple a perfect ' bas bleu,' or Lancashire blue-stocking; and his Lovely Meg a dirty red garter. Further I dare not report.

THE

RULES AND REGULATIONS

OF A

FLORISTS' SOCIETY.

I HERE beg to present the reader, by way of Appendix, with the substance at least of the Rules and Regulations of two Societies of Florists, which were some years ago instituted at Islington and Chelsea, for encouraging the cultivation of Auriculas, Pinks, and Carnations. I do this in the hope that the same will not be unacceptable to the majority of my readers, to the young Florists in particular, who may be unacquainted with the nature of such institutions, and therefore desirous of obtaining some information respecting them; they will also serve as a ready precedent to refer to for the establishing of rules for any new society elsewhere.

There are several others of the same description

in the neighbourhood of London; but these two were not only the most numerous in point of numbers, but likewise the most respectable in regard to the members composing them, who consisted of several amateur gentlemen florists, and the most eminent public florists round the metropolis. The laws of these two Societies were, in fact, both in spirit and in letter, very much alike, and several of the members belonged to them both.

RULE I.

Any person desirous of becoming a member of this Society must be proposed by one of the members, and seconded by another at one of the regular meetings, and a written notice must be sent to that effect by the secretary to every member, stating the name and residence of the person so proposed; the election to take place by ballot the next succeeding show-day; such person will then be admitted a member, unless two black balls appear against him.

II.

That a president and secretary be chosen annually, on the Carnation show-day, by ballot.

III.

That the names of the members and their residences be inserted in the articles.

IV.

That each member's subscription be 1*l.* 11*s.* 6*d.* per annum: 10*s.* 6*d.* for Auriculas: 10*s.* 6*d.* for Pinks: 10*s.* 6*d.* for Carnations. Persons making use of any art, in order to deceive the committee, except that of merely dressing the flowers for the show, will be expelled the Society.

V.

That when special meetings are called to fix the show-days, or on other occasions, the secretary shall send a printed or a written notice to each member; and all absentees shall forfeit two shillings.

VI.

That each member shall pay for a dinner ticket for Auriculas, Pinks, and Carnations; but should it be inconvenient, on the day the show is appointed, for such member to attend at dinner, he shall be at liberty to transfer his ticket to any gentleman he may think proper, indorsing his name on the back.

VII.

That each member shall provide, at his own expense, a pan to show his Carnations in, agreeable to the Society's pattern.

VIII.

That all flowers on show-days shall be in the room —the Auriculas at one o'clock, Pinks one o'clock, Carnations one o'clock, precisely, by the house clock, or they shall not be admitted; and that each member pay any demand for deficiencies the secretary may have against him previous thereto, or be expelled the Society.

IX.

The committee, styled censors, umpires, or judges, three in number, to determine the prizes, shall be chosen by members present on the show-days, who shall declare, if required, that they have not seen or assisted in dressing any of the blooms since they were gathered or selected for show.

X.

Members showing flowers on show-days, shall declare they have been in their possession the last four months; and if Seedlings, that they are of their own sowing and growing. No Seedling to be admitted to take a Seedling prize after the third year of blooming.

XI.

That the value of prizes shall be presented in plate to each successful candidate on the show-days.

XII.

That the prizes shall be limited to six in number for the named flowers, and two for Seedlings.

XIII.

That each member showing flowers on show-days shall return to his seat as soon as he has carried them into the show-room, and shall not leave it until the flowers have been brought into the dining-room, and have passed round the table, beginning on the president's right hand, and returning on his left, in order that each person may distinctly view them. The flowers not to be taken away until they are dismissed by the president.

XIV.

That if any member shall call the judgment of the censors in question, after the prizes are declared, he shall for such offence forfeit one guinea, or be ex pelled the Society.

XV.

That if any member shall create a quarrel, so as to disturb the harmony of the company on the show-days, his conduct shall become the subject of consideration at the next meeting, and a majority of the members then present deciding on its impropriety, shall expel him the Society.

XVI.

That if any member refuses to pay any of the before-mentioned fines, or shall attempt to evade any of the rules, he shall be immediately expelled the Society.

XVII.

That all forfeits be appropriated to the Seedling prizes.

XVIII.

No member is allowed to show flowers on the day he is admitted.

XIX.

That no person be suffered to touch or handle the blossoms on show-days, without the consent of the proprietor, under the forfeiture of twenty shillings.

PRIZES FOR AURICULAS.

To the person who shows the best and completest pair of Auriculas, each of a different sort, not less than seven full-blown pips to each plant :

First prize.   A piece of plate equal in value to one-fourth of the sum subscribed, after deducting the Seedlings.

Second do. . . . . One-fifth.

Third   do. . . . . .One-sixth.

Fourth do. . . . . One-seventh.

Fifth   do. One-eighth.

Sixth   do. .One-ninth.

For the best Seedling Auriculas with three full-blown pips :

First prize.. . . . .

Second do. . . . .

PRIZES FOR PINKS.

To the person who shows the best and completest twelve blossoms of Pinks, every one of a different sort:

First prize. A piece of plate equal in value to one-fourth of the sum subscribed.

Second do. . . . . One-fifth.

Third do. . . . . One-sixth.

Fourth do. . . . . One-seventh.

Fifth do. . . . . One-eighth.

Sixth do. . . . . One-ninth.

For the best Seedling Pinks, laced, or otherwise:

First Prize. . . . .

Second do. . . . .

PRIZES FOR CARNATIONS.

———

To the person who shows the completest twelve blossoms of Carnations, every one of a different sort:

First Prize. A piece of plate equal in value to one-fourth of the sum subscribed, after deducting for seedlings.

    Second do. . . . . .One-fifth.

    Third do. . . . . One-sixth.

    Fourth do. . . . . One-seventh.

    Fifth do. . . . . .One-eighth.

    Sixth do. . . . . One-ninth.

For Seedling Carnations, either Flakes or Bizarres:

    First prize. . . . .

    Second do. . . . .

PRIZE GOOSEBERRIES.

Knowing that several florists are great cultivators of Gooseberries, I have been induced, for their gratification, to insert a copy of the winning berries of the year 1823, distinguished into four classes; viz. Red, Yellow, Green, and White, taken from ' An Account of the different Gooseberry Shows, ' held in Lancashire, Cheshire, Cumberland, York- ' shire, Derbyshire, Staffordshire, Nottinghamshire, ' Leicestershire, Northamptonshire, Warwickshire,' &c. published in Manchester. I beg to remark, that the summer of 1823, being cold and wet, was most unfavourable to fruits of every description.

I have done this the more readily, because it will assist many ladies and gentlemen, also, who may not have an opportunity of seeing this ' Account;' in making their selection they can form an idea of the size of the berries from their weight, and are informed, at the same time, of the colour of each.

I beg to recommend particularly, for their rich flavour, the Jubilee, Viper, Scorpion, Ocean, and the Lancashire Lass : the taste of this last very much resembles the greengage plum, a complete sweetmeat, when ripened in a hot summer.

If we may credit the account of some of the old writers, England was not in possession of the Gooseberry-tree till the reign of King Henry VIII., when it was introduced from Flanders. About the same time also, herbs for salads, carrots, cabbage, and other vegetable plants and edible roots were intro_duced, chiefly by the monks, who were ever attentive to their temporal wants and enjoyments. They were excellent judges in this respect, for you never find any of the old monasteries or abbeys built in bleak and barren situations, without water; but, on the contrary, in rich vales, by the side of fine rivers, where the fertility of the soil could be turned to good account, in the production of corn, fruits, and vegetables, and in the rearing of domestic animals, and where the waters might afford a good supply of fine fish. Asparagus, cauliflowers, beans, and peas, did not find their way into England till the time of the restoration of Charles II. This country, therefore, does not appear to have been originally favoured with any of the choicest gifts of nature, either in respect to fruits, vegetables, or flowers. Its native fruits, if they are deserving at all of the name, are the acorn, crab, sloe, blackberry, juniperberry, elderberry, hips, and haws: all others are exotics, and have been introduced into it.

Gooseberry bushes produce the finest fruit when young; that is, about the third or fourth year after planting: they should be renewed every seventh year, and well pruned every year, or they soon degenerate. The same observation applies with equal truth to raspberries and currants.

The experienced gardener is aware, that if any tree is suffered to bear and ripen its whole crop of fruit, no matter whether it be the peach, the apricot, the nectarine, the vine, or gooseberry, the fruit will be small, and appear not like the same, provided it had been properly thinned. If you wish to try what effect the following mode of treating the gooseberry has upon its fruit, select a young healthy tree, and leave only three or four berries upon each branch, plucking off the rest, when they are of the size of a pea; then give it what gardeners call an emulsion of the ' Nectar adoratum,' the ' Lac medicinale,' which is a watering-pot full of the draining, or black fluid from the dunghill. Do this twice, a fortnight apart; if a large bush, thrice, but not oftener, lest you stupify or intoxicate its vegetative faculty, if I may so express it.

When the berries are swelling and ripening, if the weather be dry and hot, water frequently, but do not saturate it too much at one time. This is the method adopted by some who exhibit berries for prizes, and is attended with the wished-for result.

If your soil is light and sandy, and soon parches, lay a stratum of rotten cow-dung upon the surface round the root of the bush: this will keep the earth below moist and cool, and be of service to both the fruit and the tree.

I do not pretend to say that the berries will equal, either in size or weight, the newly restored antediluvian cherry of the London Horticultural Society; the real ' Cerasum Ponticum' of the ancients, one of the lost fruits of the Golden Age, four of which are said to weigh a pound; but they will surpass every expectation you may have formed. Trees that are to produce those wonderful cherries, are now propagated with great care and earnestness in the Society's gardens at Turnham Green.

But alas! since I first wrote the preceding paragraph, in the first edition of this work, I have learnt, to my regret, that this said cherry is nearly all stone, and that the stone of it is much heavier and larger than that of an apricot. It is a monstrous production of the kind, it must be allowed, but it is not worth cultivating; for it has not one good quality to recommend it, neither flesh, flavour, nor juiciness. Let it be restored forthwith to the wilderness; and let the skilful gardener continue to bud and graft from the May-duke, the black-heart, the bleeding-heart, bigarreau, carnation, morello, black eagle, Waterloo, Montmorency, &c. &c.

N.

The following is the List, commencing with

THE RED GOOSEBERRIES.

	Dwts.	Grs.
Roaring Lion	23	2
Huntsman	22	23
Sir John	23	6
Overall	23	12
Crown Bob	20	17
Lancashire Lad	20	12½
Prince Regent	22	4
British Crown	20	0
Jubilee	20	1
Sportsman	20	4
Smolensko	19	14
Pastime	20	15
Top Sawyer	22	1
Superior	21	19½
Boggart	19	15
Yaxley Hero	20	2
Jolly Miner	19	23
Printer	17	12
Highwayman	19	6
Richmond Hill	18	17
Bang-up	19	0
Triumphant	19	14
Rough Robin	17	7

	Dwts.	Grs.
Elisha	17	17
Glorious.....................	18	21
Whipper-in	17	9
Emperor	17	12
Ploughboy...................	15	12
Plim Bob....................	17	12
Nonsuch	17	7
Sampson	17	1
Patriot......................	18	13
Rifleman	18	0
Lord Hill...................	16	11
Lord Ward	15	0
Cheshire Man...............	18	21
Polander	16	18
Spanking Roger	16	14
Father Betts	16	2½
Warwickshire Lad	16	0
Roman Rig	15	10
Moorcock	17	6
Earl Grosvenor	15	9
Duke of Leeds	16	0

N.B.—Heaviest Red Berry (Seedling), Foxhunter, 25 dwts. 2 grs. Nantwich Meeting, grown by John Bratherton, Cheshire.

———

YELLOW.

	Dwts.	Grs.
Rockwood	22	9
Nelson's Waves	20	9
Viper	21	4
Delight	22	7
Queen	18	3
Chain	18	6
Golden Sovereign	21	1
Cottage Girl	19	16
Invincible	16	8
Gunner	18	4
Trafalgar	16	16
Conquering Hero	18	18
Regulator	17	13
Cheshire Cheese	17	8
Smuggler	16	20
Swing'em	16	0
Ringleader	16	4
Husbandman	15	21
Diamond	19	16
Radical	19	15
Ville de Paris	15	21
Don Cossack	17	16
Bottom Sawyer	17	6
Ruleall	16	4
Sir Charles Wolseley	14	12

	Dwts.	Grs.
Ranger	15	0
Blacksmith	16	3
Tim Bobbin	15	5
Wedge	16	20
Scorpion	17	3
Purse	13	12
Bunker's Hill	16	12
Duke of Waterloo	15	0
Medal	15	2
Fleece	17	12
Highlander	14	14
Lord Suffield	13	3
Favourite	11	11
Colonel Holden	14	22
Emperor of Russia	12	19
Self-Interest	16	10
Union	14	3
Gourd	15	2
Overseer	15	12
Rattlesnake	14	12

N. B.—Heaviest Yellow Berry, Rockwood, 22 dwts. 9 grs., Heywood Meeting, grown by Joseph Clegg, near Rochdale, Lancashire.

GREEN.

	Dwts.	Grs.
Ocean	19	11
Greenhood	17	16
Independent	16	11
Jolly Angler	19	14
Favourite	18	1
Troubler	17	5
Laurel	16	0
Mountain	17	10
Elijah	18	20
Lively Green	17	17
Wistaston Hero	17	14
Jolly Tar	16	9
Merryman	16	6
Farmer	17	7
Peover Pecker	16	10
No Bribery	16	0
Evergreen	15	0
Southwell Hero	14	20
Nelson	13	14
Green Dragon	14	7
Profit¹	17	17
Chisel	13	0
Waterloo	17	11
Bellingham	17	4
Rough Robin	15	11
Captain Greenhall	14	12

	Dwts.	Grs.
Green Ralson	13	19
Green Anchor	13	0
Glory of Ratcliff	11	20
Toper	13	0
Derby Ram	15	1
Fair Play	14	0
Jolly Cobler	13	8
Wistaston Green	14	0
Nathaniel's Pride	12	11½
Liberty	13	2
Star	14	18
Green Bag	14	8
Dr. Crompton	12	11

N. B. — Heaviest Green Berry (Seedling), Green Willow, 19 dwts. 20 grs., Nantwich Meeting, grown by Joseph Bratherton, Cheshire.

—

WHITE.

	Dwts.	Grs.
Wellington's Glory	18	22
Thrasher	19	0
Queen Anne	17	17
Nailer	18	0
Smiling Beauty	17	16
Bonny Lass	18	0
Cheshire Lass	16	6

	Dwts.	Grs.
Toper	16	12
Ferotrate	16	15
Queen Caroline	19	16
Conquering Hero	11	7
Dusty Miller	16	9
Reformer	16	12
White Lion	16	$13\frac{1}{2}$
Sheba Queen	15	11
Lady Delamere	18	5
Counsellor Brougham	15	6
Bonny Landlady	15	0
Merry Lass	16	0
Queen Mary	17	2
Maid of the Mill	14	0
Whitesmith	13	7
Marchioness of Downshire	16	4
Redress	15	7
White Rock	17	15
Venture	15	1
Republican	16	12
Northern Hero	13	0
Queen Charlotte	14	13
Lovely Lass	15	18
Pillar of Beauty	14	$7\frac{1}{2}$
Honesty	14	28
Great Britain	13	0
Fair Rosamond	13	16
Beauty of England	13	$3\frac{1}{2}$

	Dwts.	Grs.
Governess	18	21
Luck's All	16	5
Packington Hero	12	21
Ram	13	19
Hall's Conqueror	13	18
Milk-Maid	12	22
Rockgetter	14	0
Fowler	14	0
Transparent	13	9
White Flower	12	6

Heaviest White Berry (Seedling), Princess Royal, 22 dwts. 3 grs., Nantwich Meeting, grown by John Bratherton, Cheshire.

NOTICE EXTRAORDINARY.

'Non semper idem floribus est honos
Vernis.'   HORACE.

To the ladies and gentlemen who take pleasure in
the flower-garden, this officious intimation is hereby
given, in the name and in the behalf of all the
florists in Great Britain.

That as much as the poor, sickly, half-starved,
ragged, disconsolate man differs from the same man
when prosperous, well-fed, well-clothed, in health,
cheerful, and at his ease, so much does the healthy,
well-cultivated flower differ from the same flower
when neglected, and planted in barren and improper
soil. In vain will the same man exclaim, ' I am he,
I am the man;' no one will believe him, scarce any
one will know him—he is the world's scorn. So it
is often the case with a flower, when in the hands of
a florist, and again when in the care of some gentle-

man or lady's bungling gardener—the flower is no longer acknowledged to be the same flower : thus reproach is very often unmeritedly incurred by the florist.

By way of recapitulation, then, be it added, that one-third fresh loam or maiden-earth, two-thirds frame-dung, with one-sixth of the whole, dried road-grit or sand, put together in the autumn, and frequently turned in the winter, will form a compost in which almost any plant will thrive in the spring and summer following; and whoever manages to keep his plants in health, and in a vigorous state of growth, will never fail to have a generous bloom. Valete.

THE END.

LONDON:
PRINTED BY WILLIAM CLOWES,
Stamford Street.

Printed in the United States
105747LV00006BA/31/A

9 780548 507339